FREE MEDITATION DOWNLOAD

For a free download of a 10-minute guided
meditation of the Self Salutation, please visit
selfsalutation.com/freemp3

AN INTRODUCTION TO

THE SELF SALUTATION

An Introduction to

THE SELF SALUTATION

How to Resolve Negative Emotions

through Mindfulness Meditation

By Simon Timm

Namaskar Press

Washington, DC

For further information contact:
info@selfsalutation.com

Dedicated to Allyson with the deepest gratitude for all the love you share with me, which has made this book possible.

"Until you make the unconscious conscious
it will direct your life and you will call it fate."

—Carl Jung

AN INTRODUCTION TO
THE SELF SALUTATION

CONTENTS

INTRODUCTION

It's possible to be peaceful and happy in virtually any circumstance. That might sound like a distant, theoretical idea—or even simply an impossibility—especially when a fog of negative feelings has descended upon you. Such emotions often have an air of destiny, as if you've been sentenced to endure them. But nothing could be further from the truth. With effort, nearly all negative emotions can be quickly resolved.

Mindfulness meditation practices have gained popularity in recent years because of their effectiveness in helping people manage negative emotions. They accomplish this by helping you create a bit of space between yourself and the feeling. Through meditation, you step back from your intense identification with the emotion, to a position where you can recognize that you are separate from the emotion you are experiencing. You become the observer. of being the observer of the emotion. This small step can make a world of difference.

Sometimes, however, the distance between yourself and your emotions that traditional mindfulness practices provide is still not enough to resolve such feelings. As the Dalai Lama says in *The Book of Joy*, "Some forms of meditation are just trying to create a state of thoughtlessness. This works like a painkiller, where fear and anger go away for a short moment but then come back when the meditation ends."

One reason negative emotions can be difficult to resolve is they are often foils for something else going on deep within you—namely, a deeper, subconscious emotion. For example, you might spend days feeling outraged by someone's behavior toward you, only to realize, after great reflection, that underneath your outrage is a feeling that was already within you that their behavior merely triggered—like fear of your own inadequacy. Because the anger that preoccupied you was not the true problem, it couldn't be resolved simply by addressing it with a bit of mental distance. To experience relief from such anger, you need to dive deeper, into the underlying emotion. That's where the Self Salutation comes in.

The Self Salutation is a series of three-minute meditations designed to help you dispel negative emotions. This practice utilizes the powerful mental space created in meditation to explore the roots of your negative emotions so that you can address the true cause of your pain, and, by doing so, find real peace.

How the Practice Works

The Self Salutation practice works by first giving you a way to quickly identify when you're trapped in a negative emotion that is actually unresolvable because it is a mask for a deeper emotion at work. Though it can feel as though there is an infinite variety of inner emotions occurring within you, I have found that most negative emotional states fall into a few main categories. I call these categories *Syndromes of the Lost Self*—thus named because when you are under their influence, you feel disconnected from your own self, out of sorts. In such a state, mindfulness is impossible.

The Self Salutation then provides you with a way to break through the illusion by bringing the deeper cause of negativity to the surface. The secret to this is utilizing the meditative space to fill your heart with the courage you need to see and feel whatever is within you.

There is a simple, powerful antidote to the core problematic emotions that fester within your heart: self-love. Self-love is the key that opens the door of consciousness transformation; because of this, much of the Self Salutation's work is rooted in connecting you to your capacity for self-love. Once you have tended to your negative feelings in this way, the Self Salutation then offers you a means to reestablish yourself in a healthy stance toward others and life.

A salutation is a respectful greeting, an offering of goodwill. Each day, millions of people greet the rising sun with a yoga practice called the Sun Salutation. The sequence revolves around two alternating, opposite motions: the forward fold and the backbend. Each stretch, or asana, flows naturally into the next; taken together, they comprise the essence of yoga. By stretching and counter-stretching in this way, you bring yourself into a place of harmony and balance.

The meditation practice of Self Salutation is designed to accomplish for your heart what the Sun Salutation does for your body. It's a series of heart asanas, if you will. It also works with two alternating, opposite motions: acceptance and assertion. As you practice, you stretch your capacity for a healthy state of acceptance of yourself, the people around you, and the events in life beyond your control. You also stretch your capacity for healthy assertion with yourself, the people around you, and in your life in general. As a result of the practice, your heart remains strong and open.

The Roots of the Self Salutation

Since the 1960s, there's been a great awakening in the West about mindfulness and consciousness transformation. Many different paths opened to Western practitioners, including Hindu monasticism, which I adopted in the mid-'90s. Spending hours a day in meditation brought me all the way from chronic depression to a place where I sometimes get written off as just one of those fortunate people who was born with a happy disposition.

For many years after I moved into that ashram, I believed that my search had ended. But eventually, when a café I opened in Manhattan failed, my life and sense of self were upended. I had to ask myself not only why the café didn't succeed, but also why I had become entangled in so much conflict and drama over the course of the endeavor.

The fiasco exposed a level of internal dysfunction that shocked me.

It turned out that my inner peace was not as deeply-rooted as I believed. I discovered that, although meditation had given me a way to lift up to a place of peace, I still hadn't learned how to resolve the negativity within me. Instead, I had just become adept at avoiding conflict by lifting up to a place of tranquility. I realized that if I wanted to better retain my state of harmony and mindfulness outside of meditation, I needed to figure out how to truly resolve the negativity within me.

I embarked upon a study of all things transformational. I studied and underwent different psychotherapies during a year that I spent doing a Masters of Counseling program at the Pacifica Graduate Institute. I found each method offered different insights into the nature of the psyche. Cognitive behavioral therapy helped me identify intrusive and distorted thinking patterns. Carl Rogers showed me the power of experiencing unconditional positive regard from another person. Existential psychology reminded me of the truth that was part of my practice as a monk: that the inevitability of death looms in the background of our minds and creates a layer of anxiety that permeates life. Gestalt therapy showed me the power of staying grounded in the feelings that arise here and now. Depth psychology helped me to see that we are each playing out the mythical quest of our self's integration, and all the great stories and archetypes speak to us because they express that inner journey. Reading feminist and womanist critiques of power structures helped me recognize the evils of patriarchy, the elder brother of racism, and to see the ways both of these evils permeate our culture and warp my perspective.

I also explored alternative transformational modalities. Somatic therapies like Core Energetics showed me how to use the energy in my body to unblock the feelings buried within me. Nonviolent Communications helped me recognize all the ways I blame others for my feelings. Byron Katie's work helped me to surface my judgments of others and release them. The Enneagram helped me to recognize my ego structure. Marianne Williamson helped me to see that love itself is a miracle, a precious gift that only comes to us when we can relinquish our ego. Paul Selig helped me to connect with my higher self. Psychotropics took me to amazing vistas but also showed me dark corners of my psyche.

I explored mindfulness and meditation from other traditions and teachers than the Hindu tradition I practiced as a monk. Tara Brach helped me find deeper levels of self-acceptance. Jon Kabat-Zinn helped me understand meditation from a clinical perspective. Eckhart Tolle reminded me that each moment has the potential for full awakening. Yoga Nidra helped me experience myself as the consciousness permeating my body.

Fortunately for me—and all of us—in recent years, there's been no shortage of work on psychological integration. Each of the teachings I explored added to my understanding of the psyche. Many helped me in profound ways. But a lesser-known teaching became the one I turned to over and again because of the way it consistently nourished me: the Pathwork. The Pathwork teachings are found in a series of 258 lectures given by Eva Pierrakos from 1957 to 1979. These lectures offered me measures of both solace and challenge as I needed them. No matter what my difficulty, Eva's words helped me to unmask what was at work in my heart in a way that brought me out of dark places and into a state of joy. Often, the turnaround could happen within minutes.

The Self Salutation is my systemization of some of the key teachings of the Pathwork, combined with a meditation practice, influenced by some of the leading psychological and personal transformation teachings of our time, and infused here and there with elements of the Yoga worldview that I was immersed in as a monk.

How the Meditations Work

Most of the meditations in this series work in ways that are familiar to those with meditation. They either help you to pull back to the position of an observer or to cultivate a one-pointed focus on an intention. But there's also an element that's likely new to many readers: expression. In this practice, you use the space of meditation to tease out feelings that have otherwise been relegated to the subconscious—feelings like the insecurity that caused anger in the previous example.

These meditations are simple and easy for beginners. As a matter of fact, I've often found that beginners find the meditations in this series bring them into a peaceful, meditative state more easily than meditations that work by focusing on breathing or watching your thoughts. This is likely because the focus of the meditations in the Self Salutation is naturally more engaging. While the practice is good for beginners, it's also powerful for those with extensive meditation experience.

The Self Salutation is easy for people of faith to integrate into their devotional practices. Sometimes people think meditation is quite different from prayer. I'm sure that for many, it is—but it doesn't need to be. Each of the meditations in this series can be infused with devotion to God and this can be a powerful way to practice them. Later I offer more guidance on how to bring God into the practice.

Getting the Most Out of This Book

I assume that some readers will approach this book as a collection of reflections on mindfulness, and thus might want to pick and choose which sections to read according to their current needs. That's understandable. But doing so could also lead to a misunderstanding that I hope to avoid. Such an approach might lead you to jump to a section on accepting others, for example, or on asserting your boundaries. Although I do speak at length about such mindfulness virtues, this book is different from most books on personal development or spirituality because the route I offer to attain such states is quite different from the standard path. Conventional wisdom is that if you just embrace a virtue by utilizing your will at first—because you know it's the right thing to do—at some later point, the virtue will become natural. This idea goes all the way back to Aristotle, was worked into the Christian worldview by Aquinas, and is still taught by success gurus of many stripes today. That is not at all the process here.

The Self Salutation is not a practice meant to help you mold yourself into a better person through the force of will. Embracing virtues like forgiveness because they are the "right thing" to do has resulted in great damage for many people. In fact, that's the fundamental error that the Self Salutation was created to correct. This practice is rooted instead, in the idea that you have all the virtues within you naturally. You have inherent goodness, wisdom, and strength within you. All that is needed is a way to clear away the layers of defenses and fears that prevent you from manifesting your true self.

To understand the Self Salutation practice completely, therefore, I recommend reading the book from start to finish. Later, as you work with the meditations, it may help to return to different sections from time to time, because after you have practiced the meditations and absorbed the book's teachings, you may approach the specific chapters with a different understanding.

We live in precarious times. At this moment in history, this period of unprecedented challenges in society, there is nothing more urgently needed than for each of us to resolve the negativity within us so that we can defeat the hatred that threatens our world. May this book help you in that quest.

PART I

THE SYNDROMES OF
THE LOST SELF

*How Negative Emotions Alienate
Us from Our True Selves*

1. A MONK'S FATAL FLAW

How My Life as a Monk Came to an End

People always ask me what it was like to be a monk. For years I answered that question by going into a litany of the sacrifices the life entailed. How there was a military-like discipline; I woke up by four or so every morning and attended a five-hour meditation and worship. There were no days off. Sure, if I was sick I could sleep in, but I couldn't just set aside the gig for a weekend and pick everything back up on Monday. Sometimes I launched into a list of the things I did without. How I had no bank account, no salary, no savings. I didn't party, drink, or listen to non-devotional music. I didn't watch TV or movies. All my possessions could be packed into a duffle bag. Of course the most drastic sacrifice of all was that there was no sex. Really? None at all? (The bolder folks always push for full disclosure on that one.) That's right. Nada.

My description never seemed to satisfy people, though. At best I torched their idyllic notions of a serene life—and I'm sure more than one person puzzled over why in the world would embrace such a masochistic path. Reflecting on it now, I can see my mistake. I described the austerities the life demanded without saying anything about what those sacrifices gave me in return. None of what I just described would give anyone a clue as to why I loved the life as I did, why it was so satisfying. The problem is that the life was so completely devoted to the inner journey that it's difficult to convey the experience.

Perhaps a better way to understand what being a monk was like is to imagine you discover a group of people who have learned to fly. Naturally, you assumed it was impossible. You certainly never entertained the idea that *you* could just lift off and rise up into the sky. But after you meet them, suddenly there you are, up in the air, hovering above the earth. Of course, it's a momentary experience at first—to master the art you have to concentrate on that one thing for a great length of time.

But you've seen that you have the potential. The reality is there before you—if only you would grab it. And so you join this group of people in their crazy venture.

Unfortunately, flying is a lame analogy. After all, even pigeons can fly—and they're completely ordinary creatures, annoying even. So at some level, flying must be just any other mode of transportation. You'd probably get bored of it after a while. When you think about it, even walking is perfectly miraculous but nobody gets awestruck about putting one foot in front of the next unless it's a capacity they've lost for some time.

It's hard to find an analogy that captures the nature of enlightenment because it's categorically different from all other experiences. There's no underside to it. It's the final end to negative experiences, the death of suffering. But it's not just the absence of the negative. It's also a supreme pleasure. One saint in the tradition I was part of writes that the experience of bliss is so powerful that when you have just a taste of it you see all earthly pleasures as laughable—and when you become fully submerged in it earthly pleasures look like suffering. But enlightenment is even more than the end of suffering and the start of epic levels of happiness. Enlightenment is a form of altruism. It uplifts the world. It helps others lift above a state of self-absorption. When the concept of enlightenment crystallized for me it was so much more than what I'd imagined was possible in life. As another saint says, it was as if I had been looking for shards of glass but found a diamond.

So imagine flying entails lifting yourself off the ground *and so much more*, and you join a group of people devoted to the secret art. You give up loads of other things to be there and you fail day after day. But there are moments when you lift off the earth—and when you do the experience is unlike anything else because of all the beauty and perfection wrapped up in it.

And alongside the joy of those even brief experiences of flying, there's another thing that would keep you going. You would create a special bond with the others in your enclave because you're all working for this beautiful thing together—learning to fly and helping others heal their broken wings.

So that was how it was for me. I let go of everything else for flights of consciousness, for the satisfaction of living in a transcendental fraternity with a group of guys chasing after the saints.

Perhaps a short vignette will show you what I mean. In the monastery where I lived in Manhattan, I had the simplest of habits at night: I tossed my dirty robes into the bottom shelf of my locker. I never gave it much thought except that it was a little sloppy to not put them into my laundry bag, but whatever. I lived in a big room with a bunch of other guys, though, and in time a couple of the younger monks noticed my habit. We lived on top of each other so it was like that. Anyway, apparently they detected a sense of victory in the way I pitched my cloth down there because now and then, when they happened to be around at that moment, they would celebrate as if our team had just won a tournament. It was silly but there was something to it. There was satisfaction at the end of the day that was one of the best things about the life. It was the peace of having given yourself to a glorious cause. Win, lose, or draw, you had a sense that the day was a triumph.

In my fifteenth year, however, everything went off the rails. I took up a service that threw my life into chaos. Someone donated a chunk of cash to help our monastery start a business but no one stepped forward to do the job. Eventually, I did. To make it successful, I worked myself to the limit, poured my heart into the project, gave every last bit of myself to make it happen. It wasn't enough. I was in over my head. Things went from bad to worse. It tore apart our community and exposed layers of dysfunction within me that I had been oblivious to.

The most important thing the ordeal exposed was that my ability to rise above suffering was not as complete as I believed. I dug and dug to find out what the problem was, what my mistake had been. I spent hours sifting through the rubble to find out what I had gotten wrong. After much labor I concluded that the corrupting force was something that looked and smelled like transcendence but was actually very different: repression. I hadn't really learned to lift myself above *all* the negativity in my life—I repressed some of it as well. And there is a big difference.

After my life as a monk fell apart, I spent many hours in therapy and in workshops where I kept encountering the same confusing, cliched, infuriating question: how do you feel? It was frustrating because feelings were something I had learned to rise above. Why did I have to get down into the muck and deal with those messy things again? It was confusing because I often didn't know what I was feeling, or even how to find out.

With much work and a host of patient teachers, I came to discover that my fatal flaw was something we all do. Rather than resolve the negative feelings that arise in our hearts, we repress them. We do this for a host of reasons. To begin with they suck. Nobody likes to experience negative emotions. In fact, a part of us would often rather do anything than experience them. But there's more. We're also ashamed of having them. We like to think we're above feeling things like anger and fear and shame. We disprove of them and therefore don't want to admit they are there—especially if we happen to walk around in monk's robes all day. But there's also a more innocuous reason: We simply haven't learned a good way to process negative emotions. We don't have the tools to surface and resolve them.

Unfortunately there's a massive price tag for shoving negative feelings out of sight. They don't just disappear. In the realm of the subconscious they wreak havoc. If you struggle with compulsive, addictive behavior, for example, you have repressed feelings. If you have problems that repeat themselves in your relationships, you have repressed feelings. If there's an area of your life where you seek fulfillment but it remains perpetually out of reach, you have repressed feelings. These hidden negative emotions can destroy your health, your relationships and your career—while you feel helpless about it. As Carl Jung says, "Until you make the unconscious conscious it will direct your life and you will call it fate."

The habit of suppressing negative emotions is something we all develop in childhood and it becomes so profoundly ingrained into our way of being by adulthood that to stop the process—to even recognize it at work—is a massive challenge. After years of trying to uproot the habit, I realized that you can't dismantle it by attempting to transform yourself. You need to focus on something more primary, more essential. You need to focus instead on changing *how you relate to yourself*. It is this transformation that will make it possible for you to extricate yourself from the powerful unseen force of the subconscious.

The Self Salutation is a process to help you greet yourself in a new way. The essence of this practice is to simultaneously accept aspects of yourself that have previously seemed difficult or undesirable and to confront aspects of yourself that you have avoided in the past. When you relate to yourself in these new ways, you shift from a life where negative feelings have power over you, to an increasingly unflappable state of mindfulness. You learn to transform negative emotions rather than repress them. You learn to enter your heart of hearts, love the person you find there, and share that love with others.

When I left the monastery, it wasn't a graceful exit. It wasn't how I would have wanted my years of devotion to end. Fortunately, however, the cycle of life is such that each valley contains the promise of the next mountain. And so, the story of how I left the monastery is also the story of the genesis of the Self Salutation. It's also the story of me battling with just about every negative emotion under the sun. For those reasons, I will share some of that story in the chapters that follow. Before I do so, however, there is one challenge to resolving emotions that I need to discuss—which is that some emotions are simply unresolvable. At least, not on their own.

2. INTRODUCING THE SYNDROMES OF THE LOST SELF

The Negative Mental States That Trap Us

One of the most important—yet least understood—things about negative feelings is that many of them are simply not resolvable—at least not on their own. A huge number of them are simply mental traps. You can spin around in them endlessly without getting anywhere. This is part of why we just try to set them aside and forget about them. They seem to go nowhere. Much of the anger we feel is like that. It's an unquenchable fire. You can burn with it for days. You can try to forget about it but it will just seethe within you. You can act it out but even that won't bring real satisfaction. Much of what we call depression is the same. You can flail around in hopelessness and despondency for ages without seeing a way out of it.

When you're ensnared in these negative states you can wrestle desperately with what appears to be the problem. Your focus seems to be entirely justifiable: I'm angry because so and so said this to me. Who wouldn't be? Or I'm depressed because life threw a curveball at me. Wouldn't you feel down and out if that happened to you?

The thing to understand, however, is that if a negative feeling is not resolvable, then it's probably not the real problem. It's the symptom, not the disease. To get to the actual cause of your negative state, you need to go deeper. You need to pry beneath the surface emotion to a deeper emotion at work. For example, much anger is just a response to protect you from some vulnerable feeling, like hurt or pain or insecurity about yourself. Once you surface that deeper negative emotion, the anger dissolves naturally. Or take feelings of depression. Underneath the depression is a feeling of shame or grief or anger at yourself that is the real problem that you need to address. When you surface that emotion and tend to it, then the feeling of depression evaporates.

Another way to look at what is happening is to say that when we banish one feeling to the underground—like shame, or fear, or hurt—it creates another, seemingly more tolerable feeling—like anger or depression. This is what projection boils down to. Rather than contend with the anger you have at your own shortcoming, you feel anger at someone else's. Or returning to the depression example, rather than experience the crippling feeling of shame, you feel hopelessness. It's no fun, but it beats shame. Or take jealousy—rather than feel the fear of your unworthiness, you feel anger, resentment, and the fear of losing someone.

We can therefore divide negative feelings into two basic categories: surface negative emotions and their underlying emotion. I refer to the deeper negative emotions that we repress as *core negative emotions*. I've organized the secondary, unresolvable negative feelings into what I call the *Syndromes of the Lost Self*—named thus because when we are under their sway, it's like we're covered by a cloud, disconnected from our true selves. I've given the syndromes names that describe the thought pattern that you spin around in when you are caught in these modes, rather than the emotions you feel. I do that because we're often in denial about the surface, negative emotion as well as the underlying core negative emotion. For example, how many times have you seen someone in the middle of an argument claim that they are definitely not angry? Therefore I've named the syndromes in a way that you can identify when you're caught in one of them based on your thinking pattern. I've also categorized them according to three relationships that negative feelings arise within: your relationship with yourself, the people around you, or the events of life beyond your control.

It takes a bit of probing to find the true source of the syndromes, but underneath each of them is always the hidden culprit of a core negative emotion that needs to be surfaced and tended to. Fortunately, when you resolve these feelings, you can set both of the negative emotions aside, and therefore you have a sense of returning to yourself.

As I share the tale of the fiasco that ended my monastic life in the following chapters, I will do so in a way that highlights the negative mental states that became prominent in each particular stage of the ordeal. As you read, you'll see this same pattern at work again and again. The syndrome itself is a negative state of mind that preoccupied my conscious thought, but underneath that syndrome was a deeper emotion boiling under the surface. Learning how to surface and resolve these core negative feelings is the work of the Self Salutation—a process l will share in Part II of the book.

3. WHAT TO DO WITH YOU
SYNDROME

The Frustration of Not Knowing
How to Respond to a Difficult Person

One day, I decided to open a café in Manhattan. That's never been a traditional service for monks the way, say, begging on the street or meditating in quiet seclusion is. But somehow, I became convinced that it was the right thing to do. That conclusion might make sense if I had racked up extensive industry experience prior to becoming a monk. I hadn't. Now, I did learn a lot during the summer or two in high school when I worked as a dish boy at an ice-cream stand—but aside from that, my restauranteur credentials were lean.

I wasn't discouraged by these apparent challenges, however. You see, I had the great fortune of good intentions. *Lots* of them. Bucketloads, even. And, even better was that I was close to being enlightened. Within shooting range. It could happen at some point while slicing potatoes at the café, for all I knew. Or avocados—wouldn't that be fitting somehow? Of course, it might be a few years away still—satori is unpredictable, after all—but the important thing was that I was definitely close enough to enlightenment that at the very least I could figure out how to make a café run.

The first sign of trouble was a conflict I had with two of the other guys on our center's leadership team. You're likely picturing a couple of yoga dudes with long hair, stringy beards, and strands of beads around their necks, drinking kombucha. Now, think of the opposite. These two had MBAs from Ivy League schools. One was a former i-banker and the other was an executive at a major credit card company.

My two colleagues presented me with a spreadsheet of projections they wanted me to start working with. That probably sounds helpful, as I believe I've already adequately summarized my own business credentials and experience. But I was certain that neither of them had the slightest idea of what they were talking about when it came to running a café. I informed them that they were dealing in fiction and literally threw their spreadsheets in the air behind me. My heart still sinks when I watch the papers hit the floor.

I call this *what to do with you syndrome.*

A key element of conflicts with others is this feeling of being stuck in an impossible bind between two unacceptable alternatives: bulldoze someone with your will, or shut down and submit to theirs; let them walk all over you, or take some drastic action that could mean the end of the relationship. From a distance, it's clearly a false dichotomy. But when you are in the throes of this syndrome, the bind feels real, like there's no other way out. Often, this feeling is fueled by the fact that you've tried "everything," and nothing seems to work—though the fact is that usually, you've tried nowhere near as many solutions as you've claimed.

The two extremes are manifestations of over-submission and over-assertion. Another pseudo-solution is withdrawing. This is when you pull back and check out; when you stop being invested in the relationship or situation. We all tend to favor one extreme or the other as our general M.O., and use that coping method to avoid small conflicts throughout the day. But this builds up a stockpile of resentments that have to be addressed at some point.

Those who tend toward over-assertion often see their choice as a matter of expediency—it's just easier if everyone lines up and does things their way. They build up resentment because it seems to them that other people don't do their fair share. They tire of carrying the people around them—not seeing the way they invite dependence by always taking over. Those who tend toward over-submission develop a martyr syndrome. They believe they've taken the high road by sacrificing their own desires. But they build up resentments for having accommodated and adjusted and sacrificed time and again. In the heat of a conflict, you can get caught in a flip-flop between the two alternatives: spiteful resignation to another's will or oversized assertion of your own will. Those who withdraw simply numb themselves to the pain they feel but it doesn't mean that pain is not accumulating under the surface—and meanwhile life is passing them by.

What's Really Going On

The illusion of this syndrome is the idea that there are only these two unsatisfactory choices: you must either give up your power entirely or force the other person to give up theirs. But neither of these is satisfactory or solves the problem. Fortunately, in reality, there are never only two such choices in life. The bind is an illusion.

To get to the place where you can appreciate that, however, you first have to pry beneath the secondary feeling, which in this syndrome is anger. The energy current of anger is the power that has become blocked or twisted. To find your path to a healthy assertion of your power, you have to untwist the anger by allowing it to have a moment of expression. Then you can look for the core negative emotion in this syndrome, which is the real thing preventing you from standing strong in a way that is not harmful.

Underneath the anger is generally some fear, hurt, or grief. If that wasn't bad enough, those feelings are also often mixed up with shame. No wonder we avoid such feelings! When you tend to the core unwanted feeling buried within your heart, however, you will be able to think clearly about how to take the next step in this relationship in a way that honors both your boundaries and theirs. Of course you can hold your ground with this person and do so in a way that doesn't trample on their freedoms. And of course you can find a way forward that doesn't compromise who you are. The light switch is there. You just have to find it.

4. NOTHING TO SEE HERE
SYNDROME

The Gnawing Feeling That Something Is Off —
Without Knowing What That Something Is

I charged forward with the café. After loads of work and lots of delays we opened. Within a week of the opening, however, I realized that my good intentions would need to be augmented with something else if the café was to survive. Fortunately, everyone around me knew what that something else was. Unfortunately, they all disagreed about what it was. Arguments abounded. I realized that I needed some guidance from an experienced restaurant owner and found a business coach who worked in conflict resolution *and* had run her own restaurant for seventeen years. Her name is Carole Jean Rogers. She was a guardian angel in disguise.

One day, after I explained all the conflict the restaurant created among the leaders of our center, Carole Jean said to me in her sweet southern accent, and with a compassionate smile, "It sounds to me like y'all are fighting over money and power." My business coach truth-bombed the ashram. It shook me to the core. Part of the problem was that I hadn't even recognized there was conflict—strange as that may sound. I didn't think we had conflict in the ashram—let alone ongoing feuds over money and power.

With Carole Jean's help, I began to get the key realization that is at the heart of the Self Salutation: I thought I was transcending conflict but in actuality I was simply sweeping it under the rug. I would have a difference of opinion with someone and then think, okay, I'm not going to let it get to me. I'm going to rise above it. My meditation practice helped me lift above a lot of problems and mostly-sorta-kinda let things go. But mostly-sorta-kinda wasn't going to get me through the predicament I was in now because the the problems remained alive and kicking under the surface, lodged deep within my heart.

Of course my habit of repressing negativity didn't end immediately. Because of this, I underwent the same experience again and again: I would get into a conflict with someone. I would pretend I didn't affect me and go on with my life. But the problem simmered in my subconscious, souring my mood. Then I would be shocked and confused why I suddenly found myself upset with someone.

I call this *nothing to see here syndrome.*

We like to think that things don't affect us when they actually do. It's an enlightenment charade. We want to be better than we are. More advanced. More aloof. And because we've told ourselves we've moved on when we actually haven't, we can't recognize the real emotions at work; all we're aware of is a vague sense of being frustrated or stressed.

This is really the underlying syndrome behind each of the syndromes: they all occur when you suppress a negative feeling and project the negativity onto another person or blame fate for your predicament. Sometimes, however, there is no nearby target, and the cause of a negative feeling simply disappears. When this happens, you go through the day with something gnawing at you without knowing what it is. A cloud hangs over you and you have a feeling of inexplicable frustration or disconnection. You might explain it away with a meaningless phrase like, "I woke up on the wrong side of the bed," as if your mood is entirely out of your control.

You feel overcome by a negative state but can't pinpoint the cause. This is like when the police shoo folks away from the scene of a crime and say there's nothing to see here. But when you see that yellow tape and the flashing lights of the police car, you know there's something worth seeing!

What's Really Going On

The result of this engrained habit of suppressing negativity is that we become numb to feelings altogether. This is why therapists harp on the clichéd question: how do you feel? Like so many people, when I first entered the realm of transformation, I was unable to say how I felt most of the time. When I got over being annoyed by the question, I recognized how strange it was that often I couldn't answer it. But I really just didn't know how I felt. And yet, I had to admit that it did seem natural that a person must have some feeling or other at all times.

It's easy to feel trapped in a negative state when you have no idea how you got there. But there is no wrong side of the bed to wake up on. With very few exceptions, your feelings are not the products of random forces beyond your control. What invariably happened is that a specific event spiraled you into anxiety or frustration. It might have been something someone said that made you angry. Or you had an exchange with someone that triggered a feeling of insecurity. Maybe you saw a bill that made you fearful. At the time of the triggering event, you likely said to yourself, "You know what? I'm not going to let that bother me now." And you moved on. But you didn't shake it off as easily as you thought. And so it boiled under the surface. If you're caught in *nothing to see here syndrome*, sometimes it can be hard to even recall the event that produced the original negative feelings, because you so convinced yourself that you had moved on.

Fortunately, it's never impossible to figure out what's bothering you. With a bit of probing, you can always find out what's going on. When you move through the secondary feeling of confusion, you will uncover the core unwanted feeling in play, whatever it is. Or more likely, you will first uncover one of the other syndromes. In other words, you'll realize, "Oh, what's really happening here is that I'm stuck in *wish you'd see the light syndrome*. I'm pissed off at my boss for what she said at that meeting." Or, "I'm stuck in a *hopeless case syndrome* because I saw that bill come in and it got me thinking that I'll never get my finances together." Then you can pry under that syndrome into the core unwanted emotion at the heart of the matter.

I categorize that *nothing to see here syndrome* as a problem that results from the way you relate to yourself, because it's the act of denial that's the root of all the syndromes. It's wishful thinking. It's a childish part of you —and me and all of us—that hopes you won't have to deal with this or that problem, that would rather not know what's going on inside your own heart. But when we allow the syndromes to persist, we allow this childish part of us to win the day. In the final analysis, though, we have to admit responsibility for our practice of sending negative feelings into the subconscious.

5. WISH YOU'D SEE THE LIGHT SYNDROME

*The Frustration of Wanting to
Cure Someone of Their Blindness*

There were half a dozen other leaders at our center and a few other unofficial-but-important opinion providers who each offered their own ideas about why the café wasn't working and what to do about it. Pizza had the most votes. Dosas had some traction. I actually tried the vegan brunch idea, but it just added two more shifts to the week, compiling the financial losses.

My next step was to overcorrect for my shove-it-under-the-rug conflict resolution methodology and enter a tell-it-like-it-is phase. It was about as painful and counterproductive as it sounds. I fired off long emails to groups of people—an efficient way to alienate an entire team with one shot. I also took people head-on, lashing out at the other cofounders one by one. I remember sitting in a car outside the restaurant with a fellow leader, unloading on him while the street cleaner hummed by. I drilled him on everything he misunderstood about how to run a café. Afterwards, I watched him in the rearview mirror as he walked away. He cracked his neck this way and that and straightened out his back, trying to shake off the encounter. Another friendship swept away.

I call this *wish you'd see the light syndrome.*

When we're in conflict with people, we can spend an inordinate amount of time trying to get them to be different—or trying to figure out the perfect way to expose their ignorance. We think, "if only this person would change in this way or that way, everything would be fine. If I can just get them to see the light about this, the problem will be solved." But people change on their own free will, and such plans generally only further divide us.

When you're in the thick of *wish you'd see the light syndrome*, you can find yourself carrying on imaginary conversations in an attempt to wake this person up to what a jerk or fool they're being. But you can never land on the right thing to say that would actually shake them out of their way of being. Even in your mind, they keep responding with their confused logic, always finding their way out of the corner you are trying to force them into. And so you get stuck rehearsing scenarios over and over again, searching for the perfect words.

In some cases, you may go so far as to confront them or even coerce them into behaving a certain way. On TV, the confrontation approach often works. The lead character drops a truth bomb and tells her boyfriend exactly what's wrong with him. With that splash of water, he wakes up and course corrects. Yeah, right! In real life, he throws water back in your face, digs in his heels, and the relationship deteriorates further.

Part of what makes you feel trapped in this state is the grain of truth in what you're thinking. You probably have valid insights as to what the other person needs, especially if you know them intimately. But you're also almost certainly wrong as well—especially when you're in the antagonistic mindset of this syndrome. And your strategy of coercion will only make it harder for them to see the error in their ways. In fact, your attempts may have the opposite of the intended effect, and end up driving them to double down on their dysfunctional behavior out of rebellion.

What's Really Going On

The fundamental illusion at play in this syndrome is the belief that in order for you to be peaceful or happy, someone else has to change. This focus on changing another person is one of the greatest foils of the subconscious: Projection. In this state, you believe it's not necessary for you to change to resolve a conflict; change is the other person's job. But what we miss is how debilitating this approach is. When you think this way, suddenly, your happiness and peace is dependent on another person. Now, they have all the power—no matter how strongly you attempt to exert pressure on them. No wonder they resist change! If they persist as they are, at least they hold onto some power.

Frustration with others and the desire to change them is a secondary emotion. It's a tactic that your subconscious embraces to protect you from feeling a deeper pain. If you allow the anger to surface for a moment and then release it, you can then ask yourself a number of questions to uncover the core negative emotion creating this dynamic. Why do I find this particular problem so unacceptable? Why is this such a big deal for me? Why is it so triggering? Even if their behavior is unacceptable, why can't I avoid getting ensnared in this conflict? Why can't I disengage with this and assert myself in a loving but firm way?

When you question yourself in these ways, something is bound to surface. Maybe this behavior scares you because it's a shadow of the way your alcoholic mother treated you. Or it's similar to the controlling nature of an older brother who dominated you for years and always seemed to have the upper hand. Amazingly, the challenges we face in relationships often boil down to a relatively small number of behaviors that we can't seem to be able to respond to in a healthy way—but which show up again and again in the people we meet throughout life. You can master your particular challenges when you get to the root of the pain.

When you've tended to the core negative feeling— which this meditation series will facilitate—your adult self can step forward with the wisdom and understanding necessary to let this other person be as they are with whatever challenges they may have in their life. You can find the grace to let them be in their stage of evolution. This doesn't mean letting them walk all over you; it just means not fixating on their shortcomings. It means allowing them to be as they are and relating to them as such.

6. STORM APPROACHING SYNDROME

*The Worry Over Future Events
That Are Beyond Your Control*

The café tore apart our community for six months. At a certain point, I laid off the manager, who also poured his heart and soul into the café. It was one of the most miserable days of my life. After that, I rolled up my sleeves and became the manager myself. I stopped all my other monastic practices except a minimal amount of meditation. I worked from morning until night and learned every aspect of the business. But restaurants don't work on the lean start-up model where you build the plane while flying. You have to know what you're doing before the doors open because if people have one bad experience they will never return. Especially in New York City, where great restaurants abound. In other words, we were doomed from the start.

I developed insomnia. I would conk out at midnight or so, physically and mentally exhausted, but by 2 or 3 a.m. my eyes would bolt open, my heart filled with dread. (That's primetime for firing off alienating emails, in case you're interested.) I had spent $150,000 of someone else's money and couldn't see how to possibly make it right. My future looked grim. The lack of sleep, long working hours, and slim prospects of success started to wear me down. When I wasn't fending off ideas from the other leaders in the team, I was fending off disaster scenarios within my own mind.

I call this *storm approaching syndrome.*

When it comes to our relationship with life events that are beyond our control, one of the most common forms of negativity is to become overly concerned about storm clouds forming on the horizon; to worry about the future. You get whipped into a state of pessimism about things beyond your control. You envision doomsday scenarios unfolding. The storm you see could be a financial situation, a health issue, a relationship problem, events in the economic or political world, or any number of other things. When you're wrapped up in the fear of events beyond your control, you feel small and unable to defend against the approaching calamity. Part of the problem is that the future remains uncertain, so you don't know exactly how much damage the storm will do or how to prepare for it. As a result, you rehearse worst-case scenarios that will never come to pass.

In today's world, the hurricanes we face seem to constantly get worse and more frequent. But some people are so habituated to watching for storms that they see them even on the sunniest of days. Worry drives them day in and day out, causing them to hurry from one thing to the next, fending off supposed disaster after supposed disaster. That's a tough way to live. And when people get caught in the extreme form of this syndrome, it's hard to convince them that it's their own choice because from their perspective they are simply responding to external events as best they can.

Another manifestation of *storm approaching syndrome* is pessimism. When you adopt a cynical view of the future, you're engaging in a superstitious bargain. It's as if you are making a pact with fate wherein you agree to give up some of your happiness in the present moment so that a future disappointment has less bite. It's an attempt to flatten the curve. But in reality, what happens is that you retract from life in fear.

What's Really Going On

Part of why we feel trapped in *storm approaching syndrome* is that fear carries with it a sense of obligation. It feels like the most responsible way to approach the upcoming problem. Because of the urgency, it's difficult to step back for even the few minutes needed to get the perspective necessary to respond mindfully. While the worst calamities of our imagining rarely come about, it's certain that difficulties will occur. We live in a world where danger abounds. But maturity doesn't dictate fear; just the opposite.

The anxiety that characterizes this syndrome is a secondary, superficial feeling. Underneath it, however, is a deeper fear. The existentialists (and many traditions from the East) have done a great job of revealing the layer of one anxiety that permeates life and undergirds all we do: the fear of death. But actually, there is a different fear than that at work here: the fear of life. We only fear death to the extent that we hide from life..

As with all the syndromes, when you allow the superficial feeling to have a moment and then release it, the core unwanted feeling can surface. When it does, you will generally find an area in your life where you hide, where you shy away from giving yourself to life. For example, you might discover a fear of the vulnerability that true intimacy requires. Or you might recognize a way that you hold back from pursuing the desire in your heart to sing the real song of your life, perhaps because you worry you're not enough. As a result of this fear, you hold back, you hesitate, afraid to give yourself to life with the abandon life deserves. There are risks involved with wholehearted living.

What's happening in this syndrome is that you focus on something truly beyond your control and spin out what seems to be a very rational fear or pessimism—all to divert your attention away from the deeper fear of giving yourself to life in some way. But it's all a sideshow to prevent you from confronting the deeper issue. A part of you knows you're sitting on the sidelines, not engaged in the fight for the life you desire.

When you allow this incredibly vulnerable part of yourself to have a moment of expression, your adult self can step forward with the wisdom you need to confront whatever real storms may come. Fear is a twisted current of excitement. When you allow it to untwist through expression in mindful awareness, the fear transforms back into excitement. You can then give yourself to wholehearted living in the here and now.

7. HOPELESS CASE SYNDROME

The Feeling of Dejection About Yourself

Amidst the conflict of the café, there were a few bright spots. One was Carole Jean, of course, with her wisdom and compassion. One was a couple who stepped in with great sensitivity to my situation and really did help. Another bright spot was a server who seemed to love the struggling little restaurant as much as I did. She was someone who seemed to get my vision and she put her heart into that struggling little café. She was nineteen and free-spirited, spontaneous. She made me conscious of how rigid I had become with all my monastic discipline.

Now and then, instead of waking up worrying about some impending disaster, I woke up thinking of her. Finally, I cracked. I made a desperate attempt to break free from the pressure I was under. One night, when I woke up thinking of her at 2:30 in the morning, I texted her: "I can't keep waking up thinking about you without letting you know how I feel."

It's said that monks have one thing of value in this world: their reputations. With one sentence I had thrown mine out the window. If I remained as a monk, people would always remember this incident. They would whisper it to others in confidence. They would wonder if it would happen again. In the back of their minds they would wonder about the state of my heart: was I just putting on a show?

She never responded.

By the time the sun rose, I was in fast retreat. I resigned from the café that day and handed things over to someone who was already considering taking over the job. The young woman I had a crush on refused to speak a word to me, even to receive an apology. She felt violated by my approach.

What ensued was the wrath of shame. Not just for the text and crush, but also for all of my failures with the café and the community. Failure also has a way of calling up the past; it's rarely just the most recent events that weigh on you. You feel the burden of all your previous failures, all the ways you've fallen short and lost your way.

I call this *hopeless case syndrome.*

We all have a place in our hearts where we feel hopeless about ourselves and life as a result of our failures or perceived failures. The syndrome often manifests in an area of life where you want something but think you could never get it. It's the belief that something could never happen to you, or you could never be good at something. It might be something in your personal life, like being a parent or a spouse. It could have to do with your career, your finances, or any other pursuit. It's an area of life that remains a mystery to you and because of this, you've come to feel hopeless about it.

When you're caught in this syndrome, a desire burns in your heart but it's painful because you believe it will never come to pass. You're convinced there's something wrong with you, something that makes yours a tragic story. You believe you're forever stuck with an inability to figure out how to manage money, make friends, lose weight, or find a romantic partner, for example. It may be that you have a past failure that you believe (at least in this region of your consciousness) has permanently marked you as broken, damaged goods. Like all the syndromes, you may well be beyond this kind of thinking intellectually, but this is a different logic, the kind that rules the realm of feelings.

43

In the throes of this syndrome, you end up with all kinds of inner self-chastisements: You made a mess out of that! Why can't you get it together? What kind of man or woman are you? You should have done this better. You should have learned that by now. You should be further along. There you go again, making a mess out of this or that. Never could figure that out, could you?

The thoughts themselves are so unbearable that they are often only semi-conscious. Rather than thinking them, you simply feel despondent. But if you can take the time to translate that despondency into precise language this is what you would find.

What's Really Going On

Underneath the secondary feeling of hopelessness is the most painful part of the psyche to uncover: shame. Because this is the most unbearable of all feelings, we try our best to never look there. But because we never look there, shame can grow unchecked and do great damage within you. Those who have succeeded in building up a persona of confidence only make such feelings harder to discover. But there is a world of difference between the confidence of someone practiced at psyching themselves into the state, and those who manifest it as a result of having resolved these debilitating feelings.

Feelings of shame emerge from a corner of your psyche where a Judge resides who issues verdicts on all of your actions. Because the verdicts are so painful to hear, you sequester them to the murky realm of the subconscious and therefore never fully examine them. Kept out of sight, these judgments also retain their power.

Like someone who communicates with a look, the Judge dwells in a pre-thought realm of feeling. That's why the presence of the Judge is often only recognizable by the telltale mark of hopelessness. The Judge arrests you by claiming to represent one of the most important parts of your psyche: your conscience. It's this mantle of moral authority that gives it so much power, why its verdicts go unquestioned. The Judge only wants what's right, what's best for you, the highest moral standards. Or so it seems.

There are many ways to recognize the illusion that the Judge represents in your conscience. To begin with, the court of the Judge is seldom just. It offers draconian sentences for petty misdemeanors. The rulings may be rooted in moral edicts, but how just are the rulings themselves? Would you tolerate someone else assessing you the way your Judge does? Likely not.

The Judge also loves to dredge up failures from the past, trying you over and again for the same crime because one shortcoming on its own is rarely enough to warrant its harsh verdicts. Furthermore, the Judge presents a skewed version of history—one that omits important details, exaggerates faults while ignoring virtues, makes complex events appear black and white, and always holds you up to impossibly high standards. But the most devastating part of these judgments is their finality. It's not that you have failed; it's that *you are a failure*. The Judge isn't judging your actions but your soul.

Learning to distinguish between the Judge and your moral conscience is an essential step in the process of transformation. You can recognize the Judge by looking for a strict and punitive moral code that's divorced from the far greater law of life—that of love. Where the law of love reigns, mercy also resides. And justice without mercy is never truly just. Your true conscience—the voice of your higher self, your true self—will always speak with love. When there is a hard confrontation with yourself, like a genuine recognition of the consequences of a shortcoming you have been ignoring, you may experience remorse. But you will also always feel an overriding sense of liberation at having arrived at a true understanding of right and wrong.

Part of the challenge we face in recognizing the Judge is that we live in a society that valorizes perfectionism. Therefore, the harshness of one's Judge appears to be a virtue. The first time a therapist told me that he thought I was being too hard on myself, I felt flattered. I might have even blushed.

When I speak about this phenomenon, people often worry that if they unseat their own Judge it will inhibit their success. But in reality, the success the Judge delivers is never truly satisfying. The external forms of perfection that the Judge offers are impossible to enjoy when a part of you is convinced that you need to be under its tight surveillance. Find perfection instead by letting your greatness shine forth from the depths of who you are.

To resolve this syndrome, you must pass through the secondary feeling of hopelessness, discredit your imposter Judge, and resolve the core unwanted feeling of shame within you. The key to resolving that shame is learning to become your own source of love and acceptance. Painful though the encounter is, this transformation is the greatest single key to personal transformation as I will explain in more detail shortly.

A final point about this pseudo-conscience is important: the Judge plays a crucial role in sequestering feelings to the subconscious. It's not only that negative feelings are unpleasant; they are also unacceptable. According to the Judge, they're moral failures. We learn very early on, for example, that anger is not tolerated in society. Fear is a sign of weakness. The Judge won't tolerate such shortcomings and therefore banishes them to the subconscious. And of course . . . when doing so, douses them in shame.

8. THE GODS ARE AGAINST ME SYNDROME

The Feeling of Being Handed an Unfair Fate

Within a couple of weeks of resigning from the café, I was on my way to India—the place struggling Hindu monks go when they're knocked down but not out. If I couldn't salvage the café, at least I wanted to save my monastic life. My time there was a soothing balm to my heart. I spent three months in the holy town of Govardhana, and that time of pilgrimage continues to nourish me years later. There, I was able to devote my days to spiritual practice and reflect on what had gone wrong.

After my trip in India, I came back to the states to give monastic life another go. In time, however, I came to see that the kind of transformational work I needed to do could not be accomplished inside of the framework of the monastery. I needed to stop being a spiritual leader and just be able to work on myself. And so I left.

The next year was the saddest of my life. The monastic order is like marriage in the way it requires profound commitment. All my hopes and dreams for years had been tied up with that life. Leaving was devastating. But as difficult as it was to let go of the life I had so deeply loved, there is a way in which that sadness was tolerable. It even had a sweetness to it. Grief is part of life. The thing I couldn't tolerate was how I left—and now I'm not speaking about how that failure burned in my heart. There was another pain about my departure that was quite different. I kept asking myself, with all the sincerity, determination, and commitment I had shown over so many years, why had my shortcomings compiled in this epic failure? Why couldn't I have come to these recognitions in a way that was more graceful? I felt like I had gotten a raw deal. Why had fate turned on me so profoundly?

I call this *the gods are against me syndrome.*

At some point in life we all struggle with the cards life has dealt us. It feels like our hand is unfair. This is especially common when your life gets turned upside down, or when you undergo some unusual tragedy or trauma. In those cases, it's easy to think you've been personally selected to suffer a strange and unfair fate. Frankly, I've often met people who have undergone incredible challenges. People endure things I often find unfathomable. But time and again, I've seen people make peace with the most difficult of experiences—they learn and grow, finding a profound meaning to it all.

Very often the people who undergo the worst experiences are not the ones who harbor the strongest feelings of being unfairly treated by fate. Often it's those of us whose life is relatively charmed. It's all too easy for us to focus on one problem area and lose sight of everything else because of that one thing that's not going "right." When this happens, you think, what have I done to deserve this? Why aren't things easier for me? Why does everyone else have this or that except me? The evidence seems clear—your fate is unfair. In *the gods are against me syndrome*, you feel stuck in an impossible bind between resignation to a destiny you don't want and a losing battle against it.

What's Really Going On

One reason we get trapped into this way of thinking and feeling about life is that we imbibe fairytale visions of what life should be like throughout childhood, absorbing ideas that get reinforced through the movies and TV. Then, either consciously or unconsciously, we measure our current life against the idealized dream of what our marriage or career should look like. But reality rarely measures up with the fantasies we have. This creates the frustration that life hasn't given us what we asked of it. We attach our sense of worth to the degree we have achieved those fantasies. When we don't get them, it wounds our pride. In other words, part of the pain is "how could this happen?" and the other part is "how could this happen *to me*?"

The first step is to give expression to the anger you have toward fate—or God—for not giving you what you wanted. Even if you may know intellectually that it's silly to rail against reality, an emotional part of you doesn't know that. When you allow that anger to have a moment of expression, you can sense into the core unwanted emotion that is beneath the surface. For example, perhaps there is some sadness or grief buried within you that hasn't been allowed to have its moment in the sun. For example, it took me ages to accept that I didn't get the childhood I wanted. If you have some buried wound in your heart from life that has never been healed, the wound won't just sit there. It will make itself known by triggering outer events that appear to be the exact opposite of what you want in life. This is a signal for you to tend to the original pain so that you can move forward.

If the fate you struggle with is a lack of fulfillment —like when life seems to deny you the love or professional achievement you seek—another approach may help you discover what is going on under the surface. In these cases, your conscious mind is wholly focused on this desire, hoping that it will come to you. But there's likely something else going on within you that you're pushing out of sight. Break away from your "yes" for a moment and look to see if there is a "no" somewhere inside of you. Take the example of romantic love. Even if you believe that you want romantic love more than anything, ask yourself why it might be that you *don't* want romantic love. You may be surprised at what surfaces. We often fear and repel the things with greater intensity than we desire them— although the resistance is not something we are immediately conscious of. The more desperate your desire is, and the more agonizing the lack of fulfillment is, the more likely it is that you have an undercurrent of "no" buried somewhere in your subconscious.

Life is more than simply an opportunity to fulfill our fantasies. Deep fulfillment is a birthright of life, but it may not come by the road of your childhood imagining— and it will only come when you give yourself to life completely. Therefore, if you find yourself disappointed by the reality that life is offering you, if you feel that it's not giving you what you are asking of it, then try to flip that question. Ask yourself what life is asking of you. The desires we become fixated on are often simply not that important from the perspective of what truly matters in life.

9. CLEANING MY BASEMENT

How Negative Emotions Can Control Your Life

Fortunately for all of us, the great overarching life lesson that came from my café fiasco was not that the gods were up in the heavens plotting against a poor monk in the East Village. The lesson was that there was an important flaw in the way I was going about attaining mindfulness. I had overlooked something critical. The café fiasco revealed to me that buried in my subconscious, in hidden corners of my heart, were troves of unprocessed negative feelings. Each of the syndromes describes a negative feeling that is only resolvable by digging beneath the surface emotion to what lies beneath it. But how and why do these emotions get there, beneath the surface? They get there because we shove them there.

Burying unwanted feelings into a subconscious realm is a problem was all face but it was exacerbated by my being a monk. You see, as a monk there was no release valve for me to blow off negative energy. There was a constant expectation that I would conduct myself in a certain way. This is the challenge I griped about earlier about having no days off. At the same time, emotions like anger and resentment were entirely verboten. So when I was challenged by life or the people around me, I used the force of my will to set those feelings aside and try my best to act in the ways I imagined the saints I admired would act. I doubled down on humility, patience, and forgiveness. All great ideals, no doubt. But there's a big difference between patience that springs from a peaceful heart and patience practiced through clenched teeth.

Every time I offered a virtue without tending to the vice that was truer for me in that moment, I tossed another piece of unprocessed negativity into a corner of my heart. Because I was able to find a realm of peace in my meditation practice, I kept myself somewhat aloof from the ugly, unwanted, gnarly mess of feelings that I was accumulating. That is, until I underwent the intense pressure of running the café and lost the support of my spiritual practice. Then, this pile-turned-hill-turned-mountain of negativity tumbled upon me like an avalanche, tearing down the life I had built.

Why We All Suppress Negative Feelings

My challenge was not unique to the holy order. Monastic life simply exacerbated the problem. All of life is oriented toward finding pleasure and avoiding pain. Who wants to go through the experience of actual, genuine fear? It's fun for a while in the safety of a movie theater. But the actual experience is wretched. And who truly enjoys being angry? Sure, there's a little release and a sense of power, but being angry is a horrible sensation—especially when the anger is directed at the people you love. And don't even get me started on the feeling of shame. It's the absolute worst of all experiences.

Rather than go through these terrible states, we shove them out of sight. We don't even like to acknowledge them in polite society. We prefer terms that mask the true emotion, like "anxiety." What is anxiety but a sanitized way to speak about fear? Or look at the word "frustration." The term actually refers to the state of not getting what you wanted. But people used it for so long to express the emotion that commonly accompanies that experience that the term took on the status of a feeling.

"Frustration" refers to is anger—but getting angry can be difficult to admit. And so we develop a defense system that protects us from recognizing negative emotions within ourselves.

How Suppression Results in the Syndromes

The habit of shoving feelings out of sight is not a seamless process, however. Avoiding these negative feelings does not eradicate them. The act of repressing emotions creates a second layer of seemingly less harmful feelings—those that I have categorized into the Syndromes. Since the process is essential to understand, I will spend a bit more time parsing out what happens.

Take the moment when I threw the spreadsheets that my teammates had made up in the air, the *what to do with you* syndrome. Later, when I reflected more deeply on what had happened, I could see that beneath my defiance was a profound fear of failure. The anger I felt was just a smokescreen—a way for me to avoid encountering the part of myself that was terrified that I'm not good enough. Rather than feel the incredibly vulnerable fear of my unworthiness, I opted instead for the more tolerable feeling of anger. We all do this. We choose the syndrome, the second layer of feelings, because it doesn't have quite the bite that the original negative emotion does. Anger is no fun, but it beats the crippling fear that you're not enough.

The most shocking thing about this emotional layering process is how quickly and efficiently it happens in the background of our consciousness. When my teammates approached me with their formulas and financial projections, my defenses kicked in so swiftly that it took months of probing and self honesty to even remember that I experienced a fleeting feeling of unworthiness in that moment. To protect myself from experiencing that crippling feeling, I would do anything— even cut myself off from people I cared about. And amazingly, I was convinced it was them that had the problem, not me. I blamed them for not understanding the situation and rationalized my behavior as simply the best anyone could manage under the circumstances. Only months later did I stop to wonder why I hadn't been willing to take the time necessary to hear them out and respond to them with the respect they deserved. This wasn't the person I wanted to be.

As I reflected on the fracturing of my community fracture and watched the end of my dreams for life as a monk disintegrate, I recognized that the greatest challenge in my life was really this force that seemed to be beyond my control. In my dark hour, the curtain of illusion was stripped away and I could see that all the unprocessed negative emotions in my heart were driving me in unseen ways.

The lesson for me was stark: if I wanted to build my life on solid ground, I needed to find a way to stop shoving negative feelings out of sight. Even more challenging, I needed to sort through the stockpile of negative feelings that were rotting away in the caverns of my psyche.

Cleaning My Basement

During the time I spent in India reflecting on these things, I had the chance to spend a day with the popular Kirtan singer Miten. One afternoon, in the shade of the sacred Govardhana Hill, I shared some of my story with him. After hearing about the café and my discovery of all the ways I thought I had transcended but hadn't, he smiled into my eyes and spoke the words that became a guiding metaphor for the inner work that has preoccupied me since: "It sounds like you need to clean up your basement."

In one of the homes I grew up in, we had a classic, creepy basement. It was damp and dark, with a low, unfinished ceiling and a raw, cold, cement floor. We tossed all kinds of things down there, where they sat for years and grew moldy. Now and then, I was tasked with going down there to find something and bring it upstairs. I would dig around frantically through mildewed boxes and race back upstairs as fast as I could to avoid the dark underworld. After the cafe imploded, I realized that I had been doing the same thing with my psyche.

It's easy to let a basement like that develop within your heart. It starts in childhood, with all the mistakes your parents or siblings make with you and all the ways your classmates at school mistreat you. When you're a kid, you're simply too young to know how to process such negative experiences, so you bury them and move on. Later, as a grown-up, the habit continues. You suffer setbacks and betrayals. You get rejected. People let you down. Life doesn't work out as you planned. You toss the feelings from those experiences into the basement and move on. Some people are better at processing such events than others, but all of us maintain at least some of this basic strategy from childhood: banish the unwanted feelings out of site as soon as possible. Down to the basement!

The Hidden Cost of Suppressing Negativity

The thing that our child selves couldn't possibly have understood about shoving negative feelings out of site is that unprocessed negative emotions don't just sit there in the subconscious. They rot. And because of this, any event that feels similar to one of these past negative experiences can stir up all the unprocessed negative feelings. This is why a failure later in life carries with it the weight of all your previous unprocessed failures. This is why a rejection brings up the pain of all of your previous rejections.

There's another cost to not processing negativity: it burns up a ton of emotional energy to keep things trapped downstairs where they don't belong. Look at the all the energy that each of the syndromes consumes. They each represent futile little dramas. You spin around for days (or months, or years) angry at one person when the real person you are angry at is you. Or you beat yourself up over and over again for a flaw you have and the beating itself is far worse than the flaw. Think of how much time and energy all of those secondary, unnecessary, negative feelings eat up.

If you feel that you're not living up to your potential in some area of your life—whether it's your potential for self-expression, for career achievements, or for sharing love with those in your life—that's because a great part of your mental energy is being expended to keep these negative feelings under wraps.

The challenge is that this habit of setting aside negative feelings becomes so baked into your way of being, so totally unconscious, that it's incredibly difficult to see this process at work. Therefore, it's phenomenally challenging to stop yourself from doing it. And, of course, sorting through a pile of unprocessed negative feelings—that you never wanted to look at in the first place—well, that's obviously not a task you can easily bring yourself to accomplish.

The Self Salutation will help you break this pattern of living without processing negative feelings. It's a tool that you can use to check in with yourself to determine if there is unresolved negativity under the surface and also give you a way to heal and transform those emotions. When you do this, you will free up great stores of mental and emotional energy. It will expand your ability to attain the deep fulfillment you seek in life. You will live into the life you were born to live, flourish as the person that you are.

Before I explain the practice, however, I want to take another look at the nature of emotions—but this time from the vantage point of meditation.

10. THE SPELLS WE CAST UPON OURSELVES

Emotions from the Perspective of Mindfulness

This book sits at the crossroads of mindfulness and personal transformation. Thus far we've approached the topic of negative emotions from the vantage point of psychological integration but it is important to also look at it from the other direction. This is essential because if you only look at the challenge from the perspective of psychological integration you might be tempted to think that the ultimate goal here is to manage negative feelings so that you will become more successful, achieve your great potential and, of course, make more money. Although these are certainly part of what this practice can bring, my aim here is far higher. My aim is mindfulness.

In meditation, you lift yourself up to a plane of consciousness where you connect with your true self. I like the term "true self" because it aligns with what I experience. I get in touch with a part of me that has a permanence to it, a truthfulness about it. When I meditate, I feel grounded in reality in a way that's not accessible to me when I'm wrapped up with concerns over the ten thousand things, to borrow a phrase from the Tao Te Ching. I pull back from being caught up in my thoughts and feelings, from the worries of the world, and become, instead, the person who has those thoughts and feelings: the observer. In meditation you learn to experience yourself as the pure spark of consciousness that is your true identity.

In mindfulness, as I like to use the term, you bring the state of consciousness you experience in meditation to life off the mat. Meditation is far easier than mindfulness because you only deal with you—and you do so in a somewhat artificial setting, with nothing else and no one else to respond to. In mindfulness, you contend with the messy world—with other people and all their baggage, with the events of life that are beyond your control. But the challenge of mindfulness is not the world or the people in it. The challenge is your way of responding to them. If you can bring the consciousness of your true self to all your interactions, you remain above the fray—but also authentic.

In the yoga tradition, there is the idea that if you're not connected with your true self, you're caught under the spell of illusion, *maya*. In this state, rather than identifying with your pure "I am," you identify with the temporal "I ams" that have no bearing on the true self. These are identities like: I am a man or woman. I am brown, black, or white. I am a carpenter, teacher, or writer. Maya is sometimes spoken of as a goddess who casts a spell upon those in the material world, keeping us in a sleepwalking state, disconnected from our true selves.

In short, if you're in touch with your true self you are in a state of mindfulness. If not, you're in maya.

Once you come to recognize that your real identity is that of the consciousness that dwells in your body, it becomes clear that the greatest objective in life, the true north, has to do with the elevation of your consciousness. That is, to become fully conscious of the limitless beauty and wonder of life; to hold a profound awareness of the deep truth of our interconnectedness; to walk in this world with an acute sense of both your own worth and the dignity and worth of every being. Ultimate fulfillment is the lifting of your consciousness to the platform of unconditional love.

From this perspective one huge question then arises that has been debated throughout the ages: do all thoughts and feelings arise from maya? Different schools of yoga have different answers to that question. The tradition I studied views the enlightened state as dynamic. Awakening from maya doesn't entail the cessation of all thoughts and feelings, just those born from illusion. Enlightened souls feel anger at injustice and sadness at the suffering of humanity. Such feelings arise from the true self. The problem is not the emotions themselves, then, but their origin.

In this framework, the project of mindfulness is not to transcend all emotions, but to disengage from those that don't arise from your true self. How to do this puzzled me for years—until I came to recognize the difference between the kinds of emotions that I now call the *Syndromes of the Lost Self*, and the core negative emotions beneath them. The secondary layer of feelings that emerge as a result of pushing more intolerable ones out of sight are clearly maya. They're illusory and untrustworthy—just as I saw when I discovered that my anger at the other leaders of my community was really just a ploy to help me avoid feeling like I wasn't good enough.

It's also true that there is something profound about the core negative emotions that lie beneath each syndrome. When you stop and allow yourself to encounter the true problem emotion, the one you attempted to avoid, you feel grounded and connected with yourself in a way that's not possible when you're working with the superficial, surface feeling. These core emotions may be challenging to experience and they may require processing —which we will discuss at length shortly—but the benefit of experiencing them is that you finally arrive at the essence of what is going on within you. It brings you out of Maya because it connects you with truth. It's a truth you've tried to fight and deny and repress. But when you embrace this truth you return again to yourself, you stand in reality.

So the *Syndromes of the Lost Self* indicate a state of alienation from your true self. They hide the work of the subconscious. They manifest when the subconscious is warping reality to protect you from particularly unwanted feelings. If you want to get to the heart of a problem, you need to move beyond the syndrome, so you can address the real challenge. If you want to live from your true self, to maintain a state of mindfulness, to extricate yourself from illusion, you must be able to recognize when you are caught in one of these syndromes.

Fortunately, the syndromes are not the curse of some cosmic witch or wizard; they are spells we cast upon ourselves. That might sound demoralizing at first. But it also means the solution is in your hands.

Identifying that you're under the sway of the subconscious is not just the first important step breaking the spell of maya; it's half the battle. But one more thing is necessary before we discuss the process for uncovering and resolving those negative emotions which is the second half of the battle. It will help you to understand one more thing about the syndromes, what I call the Power Paradox.

11. THE POWER PARADOX

Why Balancing Acceptance and Assertion
Is the Essence of Wisdom

As I began to recognize the syndromes at work, it dawned on me that they each revolve around one core issue: power. It's easiest to recognize this in relationships with other people, because we've long identified how conflicts boil down to power struggles. But when you grapple with the events of life that are beyond your control, you're contending with the feeling of powerlessness over your fate. And when you're caught in an inner struggle, it's a battle between higher and lower natures.

Some thinkers have recognized this and concluded that life itself boils down to a fight over power. Nietzsche, for example, thought the role of power was so central to life that he defined happiness as the feeling of your power growing. Clearly, Nietzsche never meditated. If he had, he would have discovered that in meditation you experience something greater. When you lift above the spinning mind, you don't find an ego whose greatest expression is domination over others. Instead, you find a self that is inherently in a state of love and harmony. The power struggle only manifests in maya.

One of the keys to disengaging from the power struggle is to recognize that power is composed of two forces: assertion and acceptance. These are the energies of yin and yang; the two sides of the power coin. We tend to think only of assertion as a manifestation of power and miss the fact that acceptance is also powerful. But consider what happens if I yield to you in a number of ways that please you. At some point, if you wish to continue experiencing the pleasure I give you by yielding, you'd better also yield to me. In fact, in relationships, it is sometimes the person who appears more yielding who actually holds greater power in the relationship—at least in one way—because of how the other party becomes dependent on that submission.

The reason we struggle with assertion and acceptance is that they appear to be at complete odds with each other. Take assertion and acceptance of yourself. Whenever I speak about self-acceptance, people ask: How will I change and grow if I accept myself? They fear they won't be able to excel in life without their inner critic. You might worry about the same thing with accepting other people as they are—as if it means that you're condoning their behavior and giving them permission to be a jerk. The same challenge is there with life events beyond your control. How can you accept the present moment when there is so much you wish to change about it? The forces of acceptance and assertion seem so contradictory that reconciling them appears to be impossible. This is the paradox of power.

As in all paradoxes, however, the two can and do exist together. You can accept yourself entirely as you are right now and also work to manifest the greater potential within you. You can accept others exactly as they are and also draw clear boundaries so their dysfunction does not impede on your freedom. You can accept life as it is while also pouring yourself into building the life you want. Assertion and acceptance are simply two components of power.

For the true self, the forces of love, joy and power are wrapped into one. This idea is pervasive in religious texts. Take the concept of angels. Popular imagery of angels these days is generally soft and fuzzy. But the first thing all the angels say when they speak in the Bible is "do not fear" and the reason is obvious—an encounter with them is frightening. As the poet Rilke says, "every angel is terrifying."

This is also beautifully shown in the Hindu tradition in the story of Krishna defeating the many-headed serpent, Kaliya. When the story starts, Kaliya poisons the waters of the river Yamuna with his venom, killing Krishna's friends who stopped to drink the water. Krishna jumps on the serpent's many heads, kicking them down with a force that causes Kaliya to vomit all his venom and eventually surrender his evil ways. Krishna defeats this demon by performing an effortless dance and exchanging glances of love with his dearest family members and friends:

> Kaliya roared and wept and from his eyes
>
> more poison poured 'till he was weeping clear.
>
> And when he tried to raise a head to sigh,
>
> Lord Krishna danced it down with joy severe.[1]

The story shows how love and power are harmonized in divinity.

In the state of integration, there is no divorce between these forces. The only reason they appear to be incompatible is that we have so many misunderstandings

----

[1] From Henry C. Timm's *The Banishment of Kaliya: As told in the form of a narrative poem in English*

and unhealthy habits entwined with our experience of each of them. We over-assert in some ways and over-accept in other ways. These habits are so deep rooted that I might seem like an impossible task to harmonize love and power but resolving the problem doesn't entail figuring out the power paradox in each situation. It's not a philosopher's dilemma to be pondered and solved. It's more like two muscles that need to be strengthened.

The challenge of power is learning to wield both acceptance and assertion at the appropriate time and in the appropriate measure. By "appropriate," I don't mean socially acceptable. I also don't mean in a way that will always bring immediate harmony in the external world, since we can never control how others act. And sometimes, upheaval is what is necessary for the next, better thing to manifest. What I mean by appropriate is appropriate from an ultimate perspective, the kind of choice that you will feel satisfied with when you're looking back at life in your final years. I mean the choice that will bring or keep you in a state of inner harmony.

You find this combination of assertion and acceptance in Reinhold Niebuhr's serenity prayer, "God, grant me the serenity to accept the things I cannot change, courage to change the things I can, and wisdom to know the difference." Recognizing when to accept and when to assert is the essence of wisdom.

How the Paradox Affects Different Relationships

The Syndromes of the Lost Self are categorized according to three types of relationships: your relationship with yourself, the people around you, and the events of life beyond your control. It's most important to transform your relationship with yourself, because once you have balanced acceptance and assertion in that arena, finding harmony in other relationships becomes natural. The essence of the imbalance in your relationship with yourself is that you—and me and all of us—are at once too hard and too soft on yourself. You're too hard in the way the Judge rules over you. But you're also too soft on yourself in the ways you allow yourself to avoid tending to the negative feelings within you.

As you will see in more detail shortly, the essential transformation is to flip the ways you practice both self-acceptance and self-confrontation. You need to give yourself acceptance in the places where you've allowed the Judge to reign, and at the same time confront yourself by getting yourself to face the negative feelings lodged within. This dual process enables you to make the subconscious

conscious, and thereby recover your connection to your true self. It is these two inner movements that make up the core of the Self Salutation. When you have done this you will have resolved the root cause of each of the syndromes and therefore you will have an ability to see those conflicts with clear eyes. Still, there is a way to foster a harmonious stance towards those relationships as well.

Each of the syndromes represents an imbalance in the forces of acceptance or assertion, as you see in the chart on the following pages. Therefore the second part of the Self Salutation has to do with balancing the forces of acceptance and assertion in your relationship with others and with life. You can see that the meditations each counteract the imbalance that is at the root of one of the syndromes.

In other words, the meditations of the Self Salutation employ the yogic technique of alternating between two opposite motions, the forward fold and the backbend. In the meditations, you start by stretching your ability to be assertive with yourself in the most important way—by calling forth the emotions that you would otherwise repress. Then you give yourself acceptance. Next, you focus on your relationship with others. You first stretch your ability to accept others, to let them be who they are. You then you strengthen your ability to healthily

Relationship	Imbalance	
Self	Acceptance	—>
Self	Assertion	—>
Others	Acceptance	—>
Others	Assertion	—>
Life	Acceptance	—>
Life	Assertion	—>

assert yourself with the people around you. Next, you transition to your relationship with the events of life beyond your control. You first accept your present life with all its imperfections. Then, lastly, you cultivate your capacity for asserting yourself in life, your ability to create the changes you desire.

In this practice, you harmonize the power paradox. You unravel the syndromes and strengthen your contact with your true self. You gradually develop your ability to assert more easily when life calls for assertion and accept more easily when it calls for acceptance—and by developing a heightened ability for both and a sensitivity to the dynamic, you learn to tell which moment calls for which. As you do this, you develop your ability to hold

Syndrome	Meditation
Hopeless case	Self-acceptance
Nothing to see here	The courage of self-assertion
Wish you'd see the light	Acceptance of others
What to do with you	Self-worth
The gods are against me	Acceptance of life
Storm approaching	Wholehearted living

yourself in harmony and balance. Some call that wisdom; some call it mindfulness.

PART II

THE SELF SALUTATION

How to Break the Spell of the Syndromes

12. INTRODUCING
THE HEART ASANAS

How the Meditations in the Series Work

I wish I could say the café was my rock bottom, but how I tumbled after that! It was as if a cosmic dam burst and years of karma came cascading down upon me all at once. This was a blessing. It forced me to work on myself in many ways I had previously avoided. It also helped me to develop a method for recognizing when I was under the spell of illusory feelings, as well as how to better extricate myself from them. It gave me opportunities to heal old wounds buried within me. It was painful, yes—and my work is not over. But the challenges kept me focused on cleaning my basement, and the fruit of each challenge has been a deeper state of harmony and connection to myself.

83

As life bashed me about, as I encountered the syndromes again and again in different relationships and different circumstances, I began to see the underlying problem at work and the need for a way to stop these patterns of behavior. I needed a way to determine whether I was repressing emotions or truly resolving them—and hopefully a way to recognize this *before* the feelings manifested as out-and-out conflicts in my life. I needed a way to stop my habit of projecting my anger and frustration at myself onto the people I love. I needed a way to check in with myself each day so that I could have some assurance that I'm not being undermined by the power of the subconscious. I needed to know if I was cleaning up my basement or throwing more stuff down there. I needed a way to make the unconscious conscious.

One of the great challenges with this is that you can have a profound realization on an amazing retreat or by reading a great book, but within a few short days that insight will calcify into just another intellectual idea—the brittle shell of a hard-fought discovery. Or you can go into therapy and gain immense clarity about what was truly going on in your life during that one hour, but during the rest of the week, you can struggle like a rudderless ship. I needed a better way to stay close to the living truth of where I was at within my heart.

I concluded that I needed to bring a few central states of mind into the foreground of my consciousness each day. I needed a form of meditation to not only help me connect to my true self, as most meditations do, but to help me recognize the ways I had of losing myself through what I now call the syndromes. In order to uproot my lifetime habit of repressing negative emotions within my heart, I needed to check in with myself better.

The solution I developed, very gradually over the course of a number of years, is the Self Salutation. It's a process for entering your heart of hearts through meditation, determining what the true state of affairs is, and tending to whatever negative emotions might be there, clamoring for healing. It's a way to use the meditative space to surface and resolve the negativity that would otherwise leak out into your life and wreck havoc. Because the practice is rooted in meditation, a few words about different forms of meditation are important.

How to Practice the Meditations

There are many ways to arrive at a meditative state and the Self Salutation utilizes a few of them. The two most well-known approaches to meditation today employ the tactics that I call *observation* and *one-pointed focus*.

In observation, you pull back from absorption in your thoughts and feelings. You step into the position of the person who *has* thoughts and feelings, rather than being wrapped up in them. In one-pointed focus, you fix your consciousness on a single thing, be it a candle, an image, a mantra, or something else. This practice also lifts you out of your ordinary state of consciousness.

One form of one-pointed focus involves concentrating on a feeling-state and impressing it into your psyche. We often think of meditation as only dealing with the realm of thoughts—perhaps because of the term *mind*fulness—but you can also meditate on feeling-states. This is incredibly powerful, because feelings run deeper than thoughts. They are more difficult to control and we tend to identify with them more than we identify with our thoughts. A popular example of the method meditation on feelings the Buddhist meditation on compassion. In this practice, you work to summon a state of opening your heart to others and wishing the best for them in a deeper way: may all living beings be happy; may all living beings be peaceful; may all living beings be free from suffering. Not only does this meditation give you a single point to focus on, but also the practice impresses this ideal attitude into your psyche in a powerful way.

The meditations in the Self Salutation work largely through this principle of impression. The key to this method is to refocus on your intention, over and over again. Each time you restate to your intention, you try to enter a deeper state of meaning it. To understand what I mean by this, think of when you're heading out the door in the morning, late for work. At that time, you might call out "I love you" to a family member sitting in another room. Did you mean it? Well, sure you did. But your words were probably not saturated with meaning in the same way they are when you say "I love you" to that same person after you've had a deep and meaningful conversation. When you use the impression technique in meditation, you bring yourself from the casual "I love you" to the heartfelt expression by repeating it again and again, each time trying to enter a state of truly meaning it.

The Self Salutation also incorporates expression. This is likely new to most people, even those with some meditation experience. Expression is a process of using a meditative space to allow something to surface. Most meditators naturally experience some degree of expression in meditation; I know I'm not alone in getting a lot of my best ideas when I meditate. In the Self Salutation practice, however, you use the process of expression specifically to surface the negativity that is buried within you. I'll explain more about how to do this in the meditations themselves.

A Note for Believers

The last thing I want to say about how to practice these meditations is that believers can practice each of them in the spirit of prayer. People often believe prayer and meditation are very different. They can be. But in my experience, the line between prayer and meditation does not exist. This is especially true with the tactic of impression, wherein the key principle is to hold onto a single psychic state. This state can be anything you choose. So believers can simply add God to the meditations. Rather than work to summon courage, for example, pray for God to fill you with it. Rather than work to experience self-love and acceptance, meditate on having a direct, felt experience of God's love for you. The key is to avoid prayer in the way it is more commonly practiced, as a mental conversation with God. The point is to dwell on this one intention profoundly, not to get wrapped up into a realm of thought.

Since I'm on the topic of God, I would like to note that, although I've spoken about the final two meditations in terms of your relationship to life, for believers, this is really your relationship with God. I didn't do this to avoid the G word or to be new-agey. I did it because there is often a wide gulf between what we believe about God and how we feel about God. If you're a believer reading a book on mindfulness, you've likely rejected the view of a punitive and jealous God. Even so, most of us have internalized such concepts deep in our psyche. Studies have shown that young children across cultures and beliefs think that if something bad happens to someone it's because they deserved it. So in the childlike world of feelings, the view of a punishing God still dominates. Because of this, realizing that you're bitter at God for how things went down in your life is too confrontational for most believers, regardless of their theology. It would summon the Judge, who would convict them of the high crime of insubordination. So it's easier to sort out your grievances with God by looking instead at the way you respond to God's hand in your life.

13. TRANSFORMING YOUR RELATIONSHIP WITH YOURSELF

The First Three Meditations in the Series

There are seven meditations in the Self Salutation, but the first three are the essence of the practice. They help you resolve the split that caused you to become trapped in a syndrome. The central way they do this is by helping you to strengthen your capacity for healthy forms of self-assertion and acceptance, and thereby correcting the imbalance in the way you relate to yourself.

When you practice the first three meditations together, you learn to easily surface and resolve negative feelings. In the first meditation, the Eagle, you pull back to the position of the observer as best you can. This creates the mental distance necessary to process negativity. In the second meditation, the Lion, you summon the negative feelings that are hidden within and give them a moment in the sun. In the third meditation, the Moose, you give yourself the felt sense of love and acceptance that's necessary to set the core negative feeling aside.

There is a tremendous benefit to be derived from practicing the first three meditations together in this order on a regular basis. They can be done sitting or lying down, and you can take about three minutes per meditation. If you're in a particularly disturbed state when you start, however, you might need to take a longer period of time with the meditations.

The other meditations in the series are important, but not as central to the process of uprooting and resolving negative emotions within you. They help to establish an ideal mental stance as your modus operandi and to give you a way to check in with yourself to see if you are slipping into one of the syndromes unconsciously. They can be added to the first three according to the nature of your current challenges.

To give the meditations symbols that exemplify the essence of the meditations, I've named them after animals that are thought to embody that trait. The symbols can also help guide you in the spirit of the meditation.

14. ASANA 1

THE EAGLE MEDITATION

Rise Above it All

The first step in the Self Salutation is a straightforward mindfulness meditation. This helps you break free from your current mental state and enter a meditative one, creating the space necessary for the rest of the practice. Most meditations work to bring you to this experience of being the observer but some are easier than others. I discovered what I call the Eagle meditation some years ago in a book by Paul Selig and embraced it with a slight adaptation immediately because of its simplicity, ease, and power. In the meditation as I teach it, you can count your breaths to ten, just as in many mindfulness meditations. But you add some direction to it—namely up.

In other words, you focus on impressing the intention to lift your consciousness up to a higher state. The idea is that when you are caught in feelings of fear and anger, or are simply absorbed in doing life, you are in a lower state of consciousness. The states of peace, harmony, and connection to your heart center that manifest in meditation are higher states of consciousness. So you focus on lifting yourself up above your current state of consciousness, into a higher realm.

This small addition of direction gives the mind a little more to grab hold of than counting breaths. I know there is a Buddhist concept about not striving for anything in your meditation—even peace—but that's for a different moment. Here, the idea is that you definitely want peace and so you're going for it. You count your breaths with the intention that as you breathe, you will rise above the day-to-day cares you are absorbed in, above the negative feelings you may be caught up in. You will lift yourself up to a place above it all—a peaceful meditative state.

How to Practice the Eagle Meditation

You practice the Eagle meditation by simply setting the intention to lift your consciousness up to the highest state possible for you within the span of ten breaths. With every breath you take in, you repeat your intention to feel yourself lift higher and higher: "I am lifting myself up to the highest possible state of consciousness I am capable of attaining at this moment in time." Then, when you get to the tenth breath, you stop focusing on the intention and allow yourself to be at whatever height you have attained. You let yourself glide.

If the idea of lifting your consciousness is confusing to you, try to let go of expectations and intellectual understanding and just see what happens. Or focus on attaining something you do have clarity about, like a state of peace. If you find yourself overthinking this meditation, or see yourself trying to force a particular state of mind, then focus instead on the quality of your intention. In other words, work to get more and more in touch with your *desire* to attain a state of peace and harmony with each breath. Try to feel that desire for peace burning in your heart. Focus on finding the place within you that really means it, that really wants it. Just coming in touch with this desire will help to ground you.

If you do the meditation once but don't feel like it's helped enough, try repeating it for another ten breaths. That might sound silly, since the whole point was to reach as high as you could attain at this moment in time. But sometimes it just takes a little work to break free from the spinning wheels of the mind. And technically, it is a new moment.

Once you've entered a meditative space as best you can, you're ready for the two most essential meditations in the practice. Below is a guide for doing the meditation that you can refer to between breaths.

Eagle Meditation Guide

I now set my intention to lift my consciousness to the highest state possible for me in this moment in time.

With every inhale, I rise my consciousness higher and higher.

With every exhale, I release anything that holds me back.

I now summon my will to manifest my greatest, highest self.

I am lifting my consciousness to the highest state possible for me in this moment in time.

With every fiber of my conscious being, I call forth the greatest degree of awakening that I'm capable of manifesting at this point in time.

I now summon all of my resolve to connect with the deep well of wisdom that is within me, my knowing self.

With all my heart, I call forth the highest level of consciousness I am capable of manifesting.

I reach within and connect with my truest self; I enter my heart of hearts.

I am now lifting my consciousness to the highest state possible for me in this moment in time.

15. ASANA 2

THE LION MEDITATION

Gather the Courage to Feel

At this point, you've begun to create some of the mental space necessary to surface and resolve negative feelings. You've pulled back to the position of the observer as best you can in this moment in time. Because of this, you're feeling a bit of peace and distance from the ten thousand things. You're now ready for the second meditation in the series.

The Lion meditation is the most challenging. Think of it: you've decided to confront feelings that were so unbearable that you adopted an elaborate subconscious system in order to avoid them. Now you've decided it's not worth the cost. You want to know what is going on within you. But even so, unveiling the subconscious is not a simple task. These habits are far too entrenched to unwind because suddenly you decided you want to let go of them. Because of this, the mere resolution to see what's in your basement is not enough. Willpower alone will not even be enough to unplug it. And while lifting to the position of the observer is a helpful and important step, it's not proactive enough to surface repressed negativity.

The secret to making all that is unconscious conscious, there is to summon all your courage. This is a higher target than willpower. You must summon all your courage to see whatever you need to see and to feel whatever the feelings are that are buried in your heart. When you focus on strengthening your courage, it signals to your psyche that you're ready. You're strong enough to see whatever is there. Then, your defenses relax a bit, and the truth of what's going on emerges. Gradually, the feelings that have been repressed and that have caused the syndromes will begin to surface.

How to Practice the Lion Meditation

The Lion meditation begins utilizing the the method of impression to summon all of your courage. You focus on calling forth all the courage necessary for you to see what is truly going on within you. You draw forth the part of you that truly wants to be able to process all the negativity within you, the part that no longer wants to engage in the flight from feelings—and you fuel that desire with all fo your courage.

The first few times you practice this meditation, the process of impression may be the entire experience. You will set the intention and focus on repeating it with deeper and deeper sincerity, so that you come in touch with a burning desire to live in truth with yourself. This can be a wonderful and empowering meditation. There is another element to the practice that has to do with allowing for those emotions to express themselves, but even if no emotion surfaces during the meditation itself, know that you are planting a seed. You might not find the feelings within you immediately, but because you have set the intention, those feelings will surface later on, perhaps with a friend or a loved one.

As you practice the meditation, you will open yourself up more and more to surfacing suppressed emotions. Then your feelings will start to emerge in the meditation itself. At first you should not focus on trying to surface the core negative emotion. It's often enough to simply allow the honest expression of secondary negative emotion that is part of the syndrome. Even these can be difficult to surface honestly. We don't like to feel anger, for example, because we know that it is hurtful and unfair. But the idea with this practice is that it can be helpful within the space of meditation to allow yourself to have a moment of anger. Throw a little tantrum in your mind. This will discharge the syndrome.

When feelings start to emerge, you can stop focusing on the impression of your intention and focus instead on allowing for the expression of emotion. Sometimes, they emerge like faint whispers in the distance and other times, they overcome you with great intensity. Of course, when an emotion surfaces, it can be tempting to get wrapped up in it. The key here is to learn to maintain an element of observation. Process the emotion in meditation, don't get swept away by it.

If the emotion you experience feels faint, then a little emotional judo can help. In judo, instead of resisting a punch, you engage the force of your opponent and use it against them. The syndromes all result from running away from negative feelings. So in the Lion meditation, instead of engaging in a flight from feelings, you throw yourself into them. If you uncover a little bit of fear, for example, but it's just a hint, try to throw yourself into feeling it a bit more. Let yourself feel terrified of the world, as if you are on the verge of perishing. If you sense a small bit of frustration within you, allow yourself to experience anger. In fact, see if you can feel an all-devouring rage within you, a part of you that would rip up the world if you could.

This all may sound very incompatible with a state of meditation. But that's only because our predominant experience of emotions is that of being overtaken by them. When you engage with an emotion in the meditative space, you can learn to amplify the feeling without being overcome by it. You maintain a position as the observer.

Getting to the Core Negative Emotion

After you have expressed the secondary feeling for a bit, see if you can set that feeling aside. It's time to transition to summoning all the courage you need to feel a deeper feeling at work—the core unwanted feeling that is buried within you. Perhaps it's more fear. Perhaps it's a sense of being hurt. Perhaps you have a bit of shame to encounter. Give yourself over to that feeling, whatever it is, in the same way that you did with the superficial syndrome feeling.

It takes work to maintain a bit of mental distance. But the point is not to give in to an identification with these feelings. You are not your feelings—they just have a power to sweep over you in a way that makes them seem more true than they sometimes are. In this meditation, you're allowing them to have a moment of expression, so that you are no longer running from them. Through regular practice, you learn to tease out and access feelings like fear, anger, and even shame without having them overcome you. You become emotionally fluid.

A Practical Example of the Meditation at Work

This meditation is such that a practical example may help. Suppose you are stuck in *wish you'd see the light syndrome.* Say you've found yourself rehearsing an argument with your spouse. You're churning over a frustration, and so you sit down to do the Self Salutation. At this point, the idea that your frustration could be a projection to avoid feeling some unwanted feeling is at best an intellectual idea. Most of of us don't have the presence to remember such things when we're in a triggered state. In fact, it's likely that in the state you're in, you're certain that this time is different and the problem is definitely 100 percent your spouse's doing.

You start the Self Salutation with the Eagle meditation, because you realize that at least you want to be able to relax a bit. When you do this meditation, you get a bit of space between yourself and your immediate feelings, some distance from the intensity of the frustration. Then, maybe a little crack appears in your self-assurance. You realize that maybe there is more going on here than meets the eye. After all, you do seem triggered.

Next, you do the Lion meditation. You start by allowing the superficial syndrome feeling to have full expression. This is easy because you're feeling angry anyway. So you allow yourself to have a moment of pure anger. This alone is a great step because we hate to admit our anger—especially at a person we care about. You start by feeling anger at your spouse, and allow it to spread to anger at everyone who ever messed with you or let you down the way your spouse just did. Within your heart, you rage. After a minute or two of raging, you shift to focus on finding what deeper, buried emotion might be here. You probe within your heart to see why this particular incident was upsetting. You might return to the intention for a few breaths here and call forth all the courage within you, so you can feel the truth of the matter. This also helps you transition out of your frustration.

After a few breaths focused on cultivating the courage to feel whatever is within you and to see whatever you need to see, something starts to emerge. Gradually, you start to recognize that although you're fixated on your spouse's behavior, the reason you have such a small supply of tolerance in this area is because of something else entirely. Perhaps they said something about finances and this triggered a sense of shame within you because you carry a sense of inadequacy there. Underneath it all, you're afraid you're not good enough for your spouse in some way and afraid that they will reject you because of this shortcoming. Now you can see that the anger you felt toward them was really just an unconscious retaliation. You continue the practice and give yourself over to feeling this most vulnerable of feelings. You allow it to surface and see it for what it is—a little part of you that is afraid that you're not enough. When you uncover the true negative feeling, you will always have a sense of clarity about having hit the truth. Now you've gotten to the heart of the matter, the core negative emotion.

Presto! You've unraveled the illusion, surfaced a hidden fear buried within your psyche. You've cleaned up one more corner of your basement. Once you soothe that pain with the third meditation in the sequence, you will have healed one more wound inside your heart. As you practice this more and more, you learn to listen deep within yourself for feelings that have been long suppressed. You unravel those weak and wounded spots, and thereby end the power they wield over you.

More and Less Challenging Than It Seems

This practice is far less challenging than it may sound. That's because the habit of stuffing negative feelings into the subconscious was a pattern adopted when you were a child and weren't able to manage your feelings. But now, you have the wherewithal to do this. This is especially true in this process because you maintain a bit of control over the experience. After all, *you* have have called the feeling forward. There's a tremendous difference between experiencing a negative emotion when it overwhelms you during an intense exchange, and feeling that emotion in a meditative state when you have summoned it. The more you practice the Self Salutation, the more fluid you become with feelings. Then you see that feeling a bit of fear, anger, or even shame is not the end of the world. You can let it pass through you and be done with it.

I must confess that the process is also more challenging than it sounds. That's because for most of us there's a ton buried down there. It's not a one or two-time fix we're talking about. I can hardly count the times when I've thought to myself . . . what? Again? More fear? More rage? Is there no end to it? For most of us, the journey of processing these deeply buried, unwanted negative feelings is a long and arduous one. It's the journey of a lifetime. But, oh, the freedom you gain! The lightness of spirit that comes with each step is priceless.

The Lion Meditation Guide

I now set my intention to summon all of my courage to see whatever I need to see and to feel whatever I need to feel.

With every inhale, I breathe in more and more courage.

With every exhale, I release my fear of experiencing negative feelings.

With every fiber of my conscious being, I call forth the courage it takes to recognize whatever negative feelings are buried within me.

With all of my heart, I call forth the courage needed to see the presence of anger or fear within me, and to let these negative feelings have their moment.

Deep within me, I commit to seeing whatever is inside me, knowing that it is not the complete truth about me.

I call forth all the strength I have within me to withstand the truth that needs to be seen at this moment in time, knowing that there is no need to fear the truth.

With each breath I take in, I become more and more fearless.

With each exhale, I release my fear of negative feelings.

16. ASANA 3

THE MOOSE MEDITATION

Fill Yourself With Acceptance

At this point in the meditation series, you've lifted yourself above your engagement with the moment-to-moment, and you've either surfaced negative emotions within your heart or focused on cultivating the courage to do so. The third step is now to fill your heart with the felt sense of love and acceptance.

If noticing the syndromes at work within the subconscious is half the battle, then summoning the negative feelings that caused the syndromes is nearly all the rest. Because of this, the third step might sound like an optional step, or perhaps the kind of pampering only weaker people need. Far from it! The third meditation is the most crucial step of all. Without this step, the previous step won't work. Yes, counterintuitive as it is, the second step in the series is not possible without the third. Courage alone is not enough to see what is truly going on within you. The reason is simple: The Judge. If you know you'll receive a lashing for a slight shortcoming, how motivated will you be to look within? If a disciplinarian stands on the other side of surfacing a negative emotion, waiting with draconian punishments, you will never find the courage to bring negative feelings into the light of day. No wonder we hide things from ourselves!

The solution is that you must dethrone the Judge. You must unseat and disrobe this crazy tyrant. And how do you do that? You must learn to give yourself the experience your heart most deeply longs for—unconditional love and acceptance. The core negative emotions buried in your heart are like wounds that need the balm of love.

To the degree that you can give yourself love and acceptance you will be able to summon the negative feelings within your heart. The more profoundly you love yourself the more truthfully you will see yourself. The converse is also true, the more you stand in truth with yourself, the more easily and naturally self-love will flow.

Healthy assertion and healthy acceptance go hand in hand.

Sadly, we tend to live on a treadmill where self-acceptance is just out of reach. Ask yourself: at what point in life will you decide that you are worthy of your own acceptance and love? At what point will you say, fine, I may have many things to learn and a long journey ahead, but at this moment right now, with all that distance yet to go, I love and accept myself for who I am? From now on, I will become my own best friend and strongest supporter.

The great challenge of this practice is that because we are dealing with the subconscious realm we may believe we have arrived at self-acceptance far before we actually have. So if you read the above paragraph and come to a quick conclusion that you accomplished that long ago, consider that in some corner of your heart you still hold onto self-condemnation. And it's that corner that needs your love and acceptance the most.

This felt sense of love is especially important as a healing tonic when you've surfaced a negative emotion. At such times, the practice of self-love is also a way of tending to the pain that you've surfaced (like the vulnerability described in the previous exercise). Think of those core negative feelings as aspects of an immature part of you, your child-self. Now, treat this part of yourself the way you would any child that comes to you crying. Also, remember that when such feelings surface, they are often tangled up in shame. In other words, the Judge may surface in those moments with words of admonition for your shortcoming: How could you feel anger!? How could you feel fear?! What's wrong with you? You should be more grown-up than that! Remove that Judge from the seat of power. You had a human moment. You felt some fear or anger. You have flaws and ways you need to grow. But you deserve your own affection.

How to Practice the Meditation

While the beautiful message of self-love and acceptance is starting to gain ground in society, I still seldom hear of it as a tangible, felt experience. Mostly when I encounter it, it is more like an intellectual exercise, sometimes even a onetime event. That's a great start. But far more powerful than this is when you can actually fill yourself with the feeling-state of love and acceptance in the same way that you shower love on another person. Therefore, the key to this meditation is learning the art of cultivating an actual felt experience. You must go deep into your heart of hearts and fill yourself with the feeling of unconditional acceptance.

Once you learn to cultivate the experience of love within your heart, this meditation comes easily. You simply *turn on the love* and dwell in the current of love within you. To learn how to do this, however, you may need to approach the meditation from a different starting point.

One way to learn how to fill yourself with the felt experience of love is to think of a person in your life for whom feelings of love flow easiest. Allow your heart to expand with all the love you have for that person, all those warm feelings. Think of what it would be like to give them a big warm hug where you pass that love to them. Now, take those feelings you have generated in your heart and focus them upon yourself, as if you're saying, "and I love you, too."

Another way to fill yourself with self-love and acceptance is to remember a moment from your childhood where you experienced pain. Think of that little kid and give them all the love, acceptance, and assurance that you wish you could have received then. A photo of yourself as a kid can help you access these feelings, because photos often capture a child's insecurity or fear.

A third way to cultivate the felt experience of self-love is to focus on your intention, and allow that intention to guide you into the state. To do this, you can simply repeat the language in the meditation guide I have provided below, while meaning it more and more with each breath. This can feel a little like groping in the dark, and you may wonder if you will arrive at the feeling at all. But if you give it a little time and experiment with it, it will work. There is a current of love in your heart and if you set the intention, you will find it.

An Example of the Meditation at Work

Suppose you're upset because you made a blunder at work—the same one you've made several times before. All afternoon, you've had a dreadful feeling that you'll be stuck in this rut forever—always making stupid mistakes like the one you just did. Then you realize—oh... this sounds like hopeless case syndrome. Maybe I'm caught in an illusion, a negative state that I can process and set aside. So you start the Self Salutation. When you start the practice, you might feel disconnected from the concept. It's something you read about a few weeks ago and got excited about, but right now the idea seems all too theoretical. Still, you do the Eagle meditation and this creates a bit of distance between yourself and the negative feelings. Then you do the Lion meditation and you surface the hopeless feeling that is underneath the defeatist self-talk—all the work of the Judge. Beneath it all you discover that part of you that's like the child crying alone in his bed, confused and afraid that he won't ever be able to make his way in the adult world because there appears to be something horribly wrong with, him—maybe something irredeemable.

Now you set about to try the third meditation, the Moose. At first, self-acceptance is just an idea; some words you say to yourself. Part of you is still identifying with the Judge: you're thinking, I should have known better! How can I have done that *again*? But with each breath that you take, you attempt to enter a state of genuine self-acceptance and love. As you do this, your heart opens more and more, and gradually, you begin to mean it. The state of acceptance fills you and the dread dissipates. The more you work with the practice, the more readily you will be able to enter into and allow your being to resonate in a state of acceptance and love.

The beauty of this practice is that, as you learn to tap into the wellspring of your own acceptance, you become more and more liberated from the need to seek it from others. Then you can see the subtext of life—how we spend our days going from one person to another, asking, can you please accept me? Will you please give me some love? Am I worthy of love? This meditation frees you up from this need and gives you the ability to share your love more with those around you.

This meditation is named for the moose because Native Americans have identified moose as exemplars of self-acceptance. That's a hard one to verify but somehow it fits. When you tap into the energy of the moose, you'll see there's something sage-like about them. Perhaps they know this secret. If you try nothing else in this book, please try this meditation. It's the key that will unlock the door to the rest of the process, but it's more than that. It's the revolutionary practice that is needed in this world now more than ever.

The Moose Meditation Guide

I now set my intention to fill myself with a felt experience of unconditional acceptance.

With every inhale, I breath in a deeper level of self-acceptance.

With every exhale, I release myself more and more for my shortcomings.

With every fiber of my conscious being, I release myself entirely for not yet being the person that I think I should be or want to be.

In the deepest core of my heart, I give myself complete acceptance in this moment for the person I am right now.

With all my sincerity, I give myself complete and unconditional acceptance, knowing that whatever mistakes I made were made in ignorance.

I summon an experience of complete acceptance in this moment, regardless of the lessons that may lie ahead, regardless of the ways I need to change and grow.

With each breath I take in, I fill myself more and more with the felt sense of love and acceptance.

17. STAYING ALIGNED
WITH OTHERS AND LIFE

The Last Four Meditations in the Series

The last four meditations in the Self Salutation help to steep your psyche in a healthy approach to your relationship with others and with the events of life beyond your control. You balance the forces of acceptance and assertion by strengthening your commitment to their most healthy expressions. In the fourth meditation, you take the harmony and unconditional love you have manifested within yourself and share it with the people around you by setting them free, releasing any claims you're making upon them. You then reinforce your sense of dignity and worth, so that you're standing in your power in all your relationships. Next, you turn your attention to your life in general, and embrace your present life situation with all of its imperfections, so that you can better perceive the deeper perfection in life. Lastly, you deepen your resolve to give yourself wholeheartedly to each minute of your day, your determination to create the life you wish for yourself.

The meditations are in one sense antidotes to the syndromes, but it's important to stress that the point of these meditations is not to superimpose an "enlightened" response on top of a syndrome. If you attempt to jump to these meditations when you are caught in a syndrome, it won't help you to break free. In fact, it will just add a layer of repression to the problem—the very thing this process is meant to undo. The way to get out of the fog of each syndrome is always through the first three meditations of the practice.

The final four meditations are therefore simply a way to strengthen a healthy mentality within you. The challenge of harmonizing the opposing forces of acceptance and assertion in those relationships is a great one—especially because we've become habituated to ways of responding to others and life that are unhealthy. Spending time to balance these opposing forces can help to stay more attuned to when you slip out of balance.

A Way to Check In

The final four meditations can also serve as a means of doing an inventory. As you do these meditations, you can also ask yourself—do I have resistance to impressing this ideal within my heart? If so, what is that resistance? In other words, although the Lion is the primary meditation that works with expression, it's good to allow for a bit of expression into the other meditations as well.

Suppose you sit down one morning and are not conscious of any particular tension in your life. You do the Lion meditation and you don't notice any negative feelings rising to the surface. You experience it as simply an exercise in strengthening your intention to summon the courage needed to see within you—an empowering meditation on its own. It may be that you don't have anything going on within you that needs to be tended to. Wonderful! But our desire to be free of negativity is so profound that we can easily fool ourselves into pronouncing a clean bill of health when that's not the case. It can help, therefore, to check for negativity within you as your go through the rest of the meditations. You do this by listening within yourself to see if there is something that needs to be expressed when you get to the meditations that have to do with others and life. The sure sign of this is when you resist impressing the positive state into your psyche. For example, when you meditate on setting the people in your life free, are you able to give yourself wholeheartedly to that ideal? Or are you ambivalent? If you're not able to give yourself to that meditation joyfully, then it's likely that you're holding onto a frustration with someone in your life. Or when you're doing the meditation on surrendering yourself to life, do you have a hard time feeling surrendered? If so, then probably you have some resentment building in your heart about your current state of affairs. Both examples are indications that you have some negativity that you need to surface and express. When you discover this, you can pivot to the Lion meditation and see if you can surface that negativity.

18. ASANA 4

THE DOG MEDITATION

Set the People Free

The two meditations in the Self Salutation that enhance your capacity for acceptance and assertion with the people around you are the Dog and Elephant. The first of these is the Dog meditation, which focuses on acceptance. Recall that *wish you'd see the light syndrome* is the experience of trying to figure out how to get someone else to change or recognize the error of their ways. You think, if only I could make them see what a jerk they're being, they would change! Of course, in the end, this syndrome is nothing more than a vain attempt to control the people around you. Because of this, it's an imbalance in the realm of assertion. You're asserting yourself into something that is none your business—namely, who this other person should be.

Through the first three meditations in the Self Salutation, you can come to uncover what is truly going on in *wish you'd see the light syndrome,* which is generally that underneath the anger you feel towards this person is a fear you have about your own vulnerability. Once you process these feelings you can see the other person in your conflict for the person they are. Yes, they may have shortcomings, yes, they may be acting out of their own fear or anger. Yes, they may be small-minded or caught up in their stuff. But whatever their trip may be, you can simply accept that that's where they are in their life's journey.

The Dog meditation serves to help to balance *wish you'd see the light syndrome*, and to free yourself of the tendency to try to change others, by strengthening your capacity to accept them just the way they are. It's named for the dog, because dogs are loved for their unconditional acceptance of people.

The ultimate stance to have toward the people around you is the same position of complete acceptance and love that you work to give yourself in the Moose meditation: to place no demands on them, to set them free. It may sound radical to accept people as there are, full stop, but the truth is that other people's problems are exactly that. This doesn't mean you can't set your boundaries, that you have to let them walk all over you. It means accepting them entirely for who they are and where they are on their journey.

There are plenty of reasons to adopt this stance. Conflicts are bound to emerge with people in your life because, simply put, they're human beings. Whether they show it or know it or not, they are simply groping in the dark in life, just as you are. Because they are in the dark, they might kick you, punch you, smack you, and jab you—often without intending or realizing the effect they have on you, and without showing any signs of remorse. Or maybe they know perfectly well what they are doing, and they don't seem to care—but isn't that just another layer of blindness?

I'm not a betting man, but I'm willing to bet on one thing: if you take someone whose behavior is driving you crazy and you are able to dig to the root cause of whatever it is they are doing, what you'll find is a bundle of pain buried in their heart. And what's the solution to that pain? What will heal that pain? The solution is someone's unconditional love. So the question is . . . why not yours? Okay, fine, if it's your colleague at work, then your love and acceptance might not be able to flow toward them in a way that would be the ultimate solution they need. But even so, you might be amazed at how your release of them can create a new path forward for them. And in the meantime, it will set you free.

How to Practice the Meditation

The meditation on setting others free of any claim you have upon them flows naturally from the Moose meditation. Now, in the Dog meditation, you work to reinforce that state of unconditional acceptance with the people around you. If you have one particular person you are in conflict with, then you can spend the whole meditation holding an image of them in your mind as you breathe and repeat the intention to set them free. If you don't have a particular conflict flaring up, you might find it beneficial to cycle through the people in your life you are most intimate with. It is these relationships where the deepest resentments build and obstruct the flow of love. Simply hold each person in your mind and focus for a breath or two on your intention to release them of all claims you have upon them, allowing them to be just as they are.

Know also that where conflicts are deepest, setting people free is never a onetime event. True forgiveness is rarely accomplished overnight. It comes as a result of making forgiveness a way of life.

Aside from your own increased freedom, there is another amazing fruit from this practice. The more you release your inner insistence that others become how you think they should be, the more they feel free to blossom into their best selves. When you no longer give them something to fight against, it helps them to win in their own inner struggle to change and grow. And believe it or not, everyone wants to grow.

The Dog Meditation Guide

I now set my intention to release everyone around me for their shortcomings and allow them to simply be as they are.

With every inhale, I lift myself above the grievances I have with others.

With every exhale, I release the claims I have on the people around me more and more.

With every fiber of my conscious being, I set the people around me free from all of my demands and expectations that they be other than who they are right now.

I call forth all of the strength within me to accept the people around me with all of their faults, knowing that I can do so and still set my boundaries.

I summon all of my strength and use it to release the people around me, forgiving them entirely for their failures.

With each breath I take in, I lift myself above my conflicts with others.

With each exhale, I set the people around me free.

19. ASANA 5

THE ELEPHANT MEDITATION

Stand in Your Power

The second meditation focused on the people around you is the Elephant meditation. Recall that *what to do with you syndrome* develops from a struggle to respond to the spoken or unspoken demands of others. This creates the challenge of either over-asserting your will or over-submitting to theirs. You find yourself convinced that there are just these two unacceptable ways to respond to them—either come in strong and lay down the law or cave to their selfish demands.

What to do with you syndrome results from difficulty maintaining a healthy state of assertion. You lack the ability to set your boundaries in your relationships in a way that honors both yours and the other person's dignity.

Through the first three meditations in the Self Salutation, you can come to uncover what is truly going on in *what to do with you syndrome,* which is generally that underneath your struggle to respond to this person is a frustration with your own ability to honor your own worth and dignity. Once you process your feelings about your own lack of worth you can set aside both your revenge fantasies and your despair about the prospect of submitting to their will. You can then envision a way forward where you assert your will without trampling on theirs.

The meditation that helps to establish a state of mind where you can naturally and easily stand in your power is the Elephant, named after some of the most peaceful giants of the animal kingdom. This meditation is all about connecting to your capacity for healthy assertion that results from a profound sense of your own self-worth. In the Dog meditation, you honor the dignity of the people around you by setting them free from all of your demands. In the Elephant meditation, you set yourself free from all the demands others place on you by fostering your felt-experience of your own inherent dignity.

When you have a tangible sense of your worth and dignity, you don't need to give in to other people's selfish demands. You can assert yourself without hurting them. You only feel powerless in relationships when you have given your power away—something you do when you're disconnected from your true value as a person. This inability to remain aware of your own value creates a need to see your worth validated by those around you. It is this dependence on having your worth affirmed by others that makes it harder than it needs to be when other people don't reflect that value back to you. When you tune into this dynamic in human interactions, you might be astonished by the amount of behavior around us that is driven by this need for validation.

How to Practice the Meditation

In the Elephant meditation, you reinforce the fact that you have a right to stand in your power and take up the space in this world that you need. The Elephant meditation is similar to the Moose meditation in that it focuses on your own self. But it is about yourself in relationship to the people around you. You can access your inner current of power by setting the intention to experience your worth and power, and then by feeling your way into it, just as with self-acceptance. It can help if you envision the people who most challenge your sense of worth. As you visualize them, see if you can feel your diminished sense of worth, and then work in your meditation to come to a state where you feel your power in their presence. Like the other meditations, this is not a quick fix, in the sense that you will not suddenly feel access to your full power in all your relationships. But it *is* a quick fix in that the Self Salutation can bring you out of a state of feeling powerless and make you feel empowered in the particular moment you practice it.

The worth of each human being is immeasurable. Your own worth is included in that. The Elephant meditation is about filling yourself up with the felt sense of that worth. It's about cultivating that as a palpable reality that you are intimately aware of. Your worth is not dependent on anyone else recognizing it. Your dignity was given to you with the gift of life. When you're situated in this truth, you gain tremendous independence. It gives you freedom from the spoken or unspoken demands others place on you. If you fulfill their wishes, it is out of graciousness. If not, it is graciously done.

The Elephant Meditation Guide

I now set my intention to fill myself with a felt experience of my inherent worth at this particular point in time.

With every inhale, I fill myself with a felt sense of my value as a human being.

With every exhale, I release anything that holds me back from connecting with a sense of my own dignity.

With every fiber of my conscious being, I call forth a felt experience of my own true value to the greatest capacity that I'm capable of experiencing at this point in time.

I connect with the deep well of strength and power that is within me.

With all my heart, I resolve to call forth a sense of my true worth as a human being.

I now summon the most profound state of connecting with my inherent worth that I am capable of manifesting.

With each breath I take in, I fill myself more and more with a feeling of my worth.

With each exhale, I release my need to rely on other people reflecting that worth back to me.

20. ASANA 6
THE SWAN MEDITATION

Surrender to What Is

The final two meditations in the Self Salutation sequence help you align yourself in your relation to life events that are beyond your control. Recall that *the gods are against me syndrome* is the resentment that arises when you believe that you're suffering a strange and unfair fate. You feel hard done by. You think that your current life situation is unfair and that you deserve to be in a better situation, have a different fate than what has been handed to you.

The gods are against me syndrome is a shortfall of acceptance. You struggle to accept past events and your present reality that results from those events.

137

Intellectually you might have the belief that life is fair, or God is in control in your life. But on the level of feelings you struggle with that idea.

Through the first three meditations in the Self Salutation, you can come to uncover what is truly going on in *what to do with you syndrome,* which is generally that underneath your inability to accept your fate and your feeling of resentment and is likely a sense of failure, some shame, and probably also grief around not getting what you badly wanted. Once you process these feelings by letting them have a moment and showering yourself with a sense of love and acceptance, you can set aside your disappointment at life not giving you what you asked for and focus instead on trying to understand what life is asking of you. Of course, like many of the meditations, this is seldom a one-time fix—especially if you find yourself in a major challenge.

The meditation that helps to establish a state of mind where you can surrender to the events of life beyond your control is the Swan, named after the most graceful of animals. The meditation works to counter this imbalance by releasing your insistence on things going your way, giving up your fantasy of what life should be, and accepting your current life situation and your history as they are. In short, it helps you give up your war on reality.

This is a meditation on cultivating your trust in the flow of life, in the ultimate positivity of fate.

When you lift into a meditative state—through these or any meditations—one of the overriding parts of the experience is the sense that all is well and always has been. There are many people I meet who embrace this orientation intellectually, but what matters more here is experiencing this on an emotional level, as a felt truth.

The more you cultivate the ability to see life in this way, the more gracefully you will move with the flow of life —even when it takes you through events that do not line up with the dream you had for yourself. The Swan is a great symbol gracefulness, and therefore also of the surrender that leads to grace. This surrender is not meant in a defeatist way that avoids responsibility. Rather, it is infused with a deep knowing that despite all the suffering of this world, the universe is benevolent. It wishes you well. The creation is showering love upon everyone at all times, and those who open themselves up to this truth can experience it as their reality.

How to Practice the Meditation

To enter into a state of surrender to whatever is, it can help to envision yourself floating down a river like a stick, allowing the current to take you here and there. Give yourself up to the current of life wherever it brings you. You can tumble through rapids and even let yourself cascade down a waterfall, knowing that you will pop up to the surface and find more peaceful waters again downstream. The intentions established in the meditation guide below can also help you get to that state.

The most essential part of this meditation is the release of any and every insistence that life go *your* way. Give yourself up to fate. Trust in the benevolence of the universe or God with the faith that a higher design is at work in your life right now. The most important thing is to be malleable. Adopt the spirit that no matter what happens, you can learn and grow from the lessons of life before you.

When you relinquish your grip on things going the way you want, and trust in the ultimate goodness of life, a miracle happens. You start to perceive a greater perfection that exists beneath the surface of life. And though you may have experienced hardship, you can come to a place where you perceive the lessons in these experiences. You experience the truth that you are not defined by your circumstances. The fantasies you cultivated of the perfect life may never come to pass, but an ultimate experience of fulfillment is your birthright. The more you can release your insistence on attaining fulfillment in *your way*, the more easily the flow of life will bring you to a place of deeper perfection and fulfillment.

The Swan Meditation Guide

I now set my intention to surrender myself entirely at this particular point in time, letting go of all of my demands on life.

With every inhale, I fill myself with trust in the flow of life.

With every exhale, I release my insistence on things going my way.

With every fiber of my conscious being, I call forth a state of complete acceptance of my life situation at this point in time.

Here and now, I release my tight insistence that things go my way.

With all my heart, I call forth the part of me that trusts in the flow of life.

I summon the deepest state of acceptance that I'm capable of manifesting at this point in time.

With every inhale, I fill myself with the strength to let go.

With every exhale, I release whatever I am holding onto that does not benefit me.

21. ASANA 7

THE HUMMINGBIRD MEDITATION

Pour Yourself into Life

While we must surrender to the way events beyond our control have shaped our past and our present, we must simultaneously cultivate another focus—the spirit of giving ourselves wholeheartedly to the life we want for ourselves, which is the focus in the final meditation in the Self Salutation. This meditation is also a counterbalance for the other challenge that arises in relationship to life, which is *storm approaching syndrome,* or the worry over future events beyond your control.

When you're caught in the throes of *storm approaching syndrome* you see doom and gloom in your future. You worry that events will transpire that you might not be able to handle—or you employ a pessimistic outlook, as if assuming the worst will make it somehow more tolerable when it happens.

While *the gods are against me syndrome* is an imbalance in your ability to accept your life, *storm approaching syndrome* derives from a shortfall of your ability to assert yourself in life. Reality may demand that we accept what is and what has been, but this doesn't mean that we must live passively.

When pessimism and worry about the future might descend upon you, they always seem as though they are the obvious and natural responses to the potential threats ahead of you. You can feel duty-bound to suffer through them. This is not so easy to shake off. Before you get to the point where you can dive in with everything you have, it's important to first process the underlying fear of this syndrome through the first three meditations in the Self Salutation. When you do this, you will uncover that underneath *storm approaching syndrome* is a childlike part of you is frozen in time. He or she is overwhelmed and unable to cope in the adult world. Once you tend to that part of you by letting it have a moment in the sun, and once you shower that part of you with a sense of love and acceptance, you can set aside the childish fears and give yourself wholeheartedly to life despite the fact that there are no guarantees in life.

The final meditation in the Self Salutation sequence, therefore, is to give yourself to life with abandon, just as nature does. It's named after the hummingbird, those mystical and miraculous little birds that flap their wings fifteen times a second and yet hover in the air in one place. The final meditation is a commitment to wholehearted living, to bringing your dreams to life. It's a meditation that helps to build your resolve to pour every last drop of yourself into building the life you want here and now; a commitment to taking complete responsibility for your destiny and your response to any life situation that you find yourself in.

How to Practice the Meditation

To practice this meditation, it can help to think back to a time in your life when you kicked ass massively. Think of an area of your life where you are unstoppable. Sports are great for this, because that physical feeling of giving everything captures the spirit. Recall that feeling. You can also use the meditation guide below to cultivate your will to give yourself to every aspect of your life with this relentless spirit.

When you give your heart and soul to creating the best life you can envision—not out of fear of some impending storm but for the sake of bringing to life your positive vision of what can be—there is little room for pessimism and worry. Yes, there are challenges. Yes, there are losses. Yes, there is pain in this world. Each of these will come your way. Yet they are nothing to run away from.

When you cultivate this spirit an amazing transformation happens: you gain a profound sense of trust in your own resilience. People who play all out—who give every last drop to create the life and world they want—aren't susceptible to worry and fear in the same way as those who sit on the sidelines. When you give your very best to life you get in touch with the part of you that knows there is nothing life can hand you that you can't handle. Even death is something you can and will endure.

The Hummingbird Meditation Guide

I now set my intention to pour myself into my life with wholeheartedness at this particular point in time.

With every inhale, I fill myself with determination to give everything to life.

With every exhale, I release the ways I have of holding back.

With every fiber of my conscious being, I summon all the positive energy I am capable of manifesting at this point in time, and offer that to life.

I summon all of my will to pour myself into life, to play all out.

Here and now, I connect with the deep well of strength that is within me, so that I can give myself to life fearlessly.

With all my heart, I call forth the most positive, powerful person I am.

I hereby resolve to give myself to life with abandon, to pour every last drop of myself into the things that matter most.

With every inhale, I fill myself with the will to give of myself to life.

With every exhale, I release pessimism and fear.

22. CONCLUSION

Where to Go from Here

Life is a series of lessons that teach us how to expand the power of our love beyond limit. The Self Salutation is a series of meditations to help you integrate those lessons. You first take a few minutes to summons your higher self, the Eagle meditation. Then you probe within yourself to see if there are negative feelings buried in a corner of your heart, the Lion meditation. If so, you process those feelings. You bring them to the surface and tend to whatever deeper feelings may be beneath them. Next, you fill yourself with the one thing every soul needs more than anything in life: a felt sense of unconditional love and acceptance. After the Moose meditation, you take a few moments to share that love with the people around you by setting them free, releasing any claims you're making upon them, the Dog meditation. You then reinforce your sense of dignity and worth so that you're standing in your power in all your relationships, the Elephant meditation. Next, you turn your attention to your life in general and embrace your present life situation with all of its imperfections so you can better perceive the deeper perfection in life, the Swan meditation. Lastly, you deepen your resolve to give yourself wholeheartedly to each minute of your day, pouring yourself into life with abandon, the Hummingbird meditation.

As you work with the meditations in the Self Salutation series, you harmonize the energies of assertion and acceptance within yourself. You establish and reinforce a way of treating yourself that includes both fearless self-honesty and complete self-compassion. You cultivate your ability to simultaneously stand in your power and worth with the people around you, and also honor their dignity and worth. You develop your capacity to embrace the flow of life even when it is not the journey you planned, while also giving your everything to bring your deepest dreams to life.

Like all meditations, the Self Salutation requires practice before you can access each of the heart asanas in an easy, natural way. The most difficult, as I'm sure you have seen, is the Lion, as it is the meditation that directly confronts our inherent tendency to avoid the negative feelings buried in our hearts. The fruit of this practice, however, is profound. As you strengthen your ability to do this, you will gain greater mastery over your emotions. Not as a result of an iron-fistedness that belies a fear of feelings, but in a fluid way that allows feelings to flow through you as a result of your ability process them.

The techniques in this introductory book are meant to give you a brief overview of the entire process. The forthcoming books in this series will delve more deeply into each of the meditations and syndromes. I invite you to visit selfsalutation.com for free tools, a blog about the practice, meditation downloads, and live online meditation sessions.

May all living beings find lasting happiness. May all living beings find the deepest fulfillment. May all living beings be free from suffering and pain. And may these words help as many as possible. Hari Om Tat Sat.

FREE MEDITATION DOWNLOAD
For a free download of a 10-minute guided meditation of the Self Salutation, please visit selfsalutation.com/freemp3

ACKNOWLEDGEMENTS

I'm especially indebted to Allyson McKinney Timm for all her support and encouragement in writing this book — and for her thoughtful comments on numerous drafts. Thanks also to my Mom, Yhanna Coffin, who not only helped me with feedback, but also, more importantly, introduced me to so many wonderful teachers that have helped me integrate these lessons—when the time was right. Speaking of guides, I'm deeply indebted to Ann Bradney for her profound example, teachings and and help. I'm also indebted to James Hannon, Patricia Haman, Malcolm Henderson, James Knight, Jac Conaway, Vyana Bergen, Cristian Graca, and Brian Gleason for helping me arrive at so many of these realizations throughout my journey. I'm grateful to Barra

Kahn for both her wisdom in my life and her helpful feedback on an early draft. My journey would have been unbearable without the friendship of my fellow pilgrims, whom I relied on for feedback and support throughout this entire process, especially Johann Diermann, Francis Guerriero, and Prentiss Alter

My thanks to Gabrielle Moss for a slew of helpful insights that brought tremendous clarity to the book in her content edit. Thanks to the many readers and conversation partners who gave me feedback on different drafts, including James Davis, PerCilla Zeno, Jim Ehrman, Lynna Dhanani, Kelsey Beth, Sari Dweck, Jonathan Edelmann, and Benjamin McClintic. My thanks to Emily Fiore for her awesome suggestion which resulted in the cover design. Thanks also to all the students I've worked with who have provided great insights into the teachings and process.

So far as the spiritual component of this book is concerned, I owe an incalculable debt to H. H. Radhanath Swami Maharaja for all the wisdom, inspiration, and training he has given me over the years as my diksha guru. I've never met a person more powerfully immersed in the current of unconditional love.

Lastly, I want to thank the many writing teachers who have helped me with the craft, starting with my father, Henry C. Timm, who instilled within me a great love for the written word—and respect for the poet. Thanks to Ron Kuka and Timur Uckun who taught me more about words than words can say. And thanks to Gladys Veidemanis, who created an oasis in a high school desert. Through her mastery of the socratic method and her love for her students, she nourished my longing for meaning and my love for writing—and how!

ABOUT THE AUTHOR

Simon Timm is a mindfulness and meditation teacher who spent sixteen years as a Hindu monk. When he left the monastic life, he embarked on a journey of psychological integration and set out to develop a way to use the powerful space created during meditation to resolve negative feelings—rather than just lift above them. The result is The Self Salutation. On his website, selfsalutation.com, you will find a blog, free materials to download, audio and video clips, and access to online courses. Simon has a Masters in Religion and Ethics from Yale. A paper of his on philosophy and cognitive science was published in the journal *NeuroEthics*. He lives with his spouse, Allyson, in Washington, DC.

FREE MEDITATION DOWNLOAD

For a free download of a 10-minute guided meditation of the Self Salutation, please visit selfsalutation.com/freemp3